Living the Hospitality of God

Living the Hospitality of God

Lucien Richard, O.M.I.

PAULIST PRESS
New York   Mahwah, N.J.

ROBERT J. WICKS
A Spirituality Selection

Book design by Lynn Else and Theresa M. Sparacio

Cover design by Cynthia Dunne

Library of Congress Cataloging-in-Publication Data

Richard, Lucien.
   Living the hospitality of God / by Lucien Richard.
     p.   cm.
   Includes bibliographical references.
   ISBN 0-8091-3998-7 (alk. paper)
   1. Hospitality—Religious aspects—Christianity. I. Title.

BV4647.H67 .R53 2000
241'.671—dc21

00-057482

Published by Paulist Press
997 Macarthur Boulevard
Mahwah, New Jersey 07430

www.paulistpress.com

Printed and bound in the
United States of America

CONTENTS

I dedicate this book to the
new generation:

Abby Marie, Alex, Andrew,
Anthony, Emily, Lucas,
Marcus and Stefanie

INTRODUCTION

*C*hristianity is above all a vision and therefore a way of seeing. Christianity offers a peculiar and distinctive take on reality, on what is really real. I am suggesting that such a vision and such a take are well expressed in the scripture's affirmation: "I was a stranger and you welcomed me" (Matt 25:35). To be a Christian, a disciple of Christ, is to see the stranger the way Christ saw the stranger and by implications the way God sees the stranger. My argument is guided by the conviction that concern for the stranger offers an originating pattern for the Christian community's orientation in and perspective on the world. Reflections on the scripture's teaching on hospitality to the stranger offer a particular lens or key by which Christians interpret circumstances and realities in their attempt to envision the whole of life in relation to God and to the other. The command to be hospitable to the stranger, to love our neighbor, even our neighbor's enemy, is Christianity's attempt to interpret the world, to say how things are, to avoid deceit, delusion, and lies. The command expresses the Christian "reality," the Christian "essence." The language of reality, of essence, has to do with a community's paradigm of reality. Paradigms are ways that communities, religious and others, identify and interpret what is real and what is not real. While there are various aspects to the real, the primary characteristic of the real is that the real has to do with the "other," with "otherness." As Edward Farley writes, "To be engaged by the real we human beings must be able to distinguish what is other to ourselves, what is irreducible to our own needs and wishes. If we cannot get outside the circle of our autonomous interests and desires, we will experience only reflections of ourselves."[1]

For Christianity, the reality of hospitality to the stranger is expressed in the meals taken by Jesus with those who were at the margin of society; here is revelation, sacrament, word of God.

The Christian reality is not simply a thing or object but the way Christianity exists. Such a reality provides us with an image that brings intelligibility to all occasions of personal and common life. It affects the Christian community's preaching, worship, ways of caring, and ethical concern. Many elements make up Christianity's vision of hospitality to the stranger. Hospitality itself is a complex category. It has much to do with the intersection of the private and the public life. The stranger is encountered in the public realm; hospitality has to do with the private realm. In the public realm our lives are intertwined with those of strangers. The private realm is characterized by mutuality, reciprocity, and intimacy. Hospitality can function as a point of intersection between the private and the public.

In the Christian tradition hospitality is the way that should characterize our meeting with strangers. The practice of hospitality was viewed as the concrete expression of love. "Let love be genuine.... Love one another with mutual affection.... Contribute to the needs of the saints; extend hospitality" (Rom 12:9-13). "Let mutual love continue. Do not neglect to show hospitality to strangers, for by doing that some have entertained angels without knowing it" (Heb 13:1-2). "Above all, maintain constant love for one another, for love covers a multitude of sins. Be hospitable to one another without complaining. Like good stewards of the manifold grace of God, serve for one another with whatever gift each of you has received" (1 Pet 4:8-10). Christians affirm that they "are no longer strangers and aliens, but citizens with the saints and also members of the household of God" (Eph 2:19).

The purpose of this book is to examine the theological and pastoral impact of the biblical command to be hospitable to the stranger. As a fundamental theological reality and symbol such a command provides the possibility of a critical stance toward present forms of existence and order in the social world. It can lead us to an acceptable model of humanhood and call us to social action on behalf of a new earth. It is an important theme for our own time, which seems preoccupied with individual autonomy and individual prosperity, and marked by a deep ambiguity, fear, and distrust of the stranger.

The world faces the staggering plight of a hundred million refugees. Millions of people forced to flee their homelands in recent decades now make up a vast nation of stateless nomads whose worlds overlap with our own. Ethnic cleansings in the Balkans and Africa have become ongoing fare of television news. Some refugees pass through refugee camps, becoming faceless numbers on various lists of displaced persons awaiting resettlement to a country that will have them. Such refugees are faced with enduring bureaucratic torture in order to obtain documents that will permit them to start a new life in a host country. Others roam from country to country. Some desperate wanderers never find asylum and are forced to return to places they originally had to flee. All have to endure the same degradation and privations. These are disaster-struck people sharing the same human impulses in seeking asylum: a desire to escape danger and to hope for a better life.

Being a refugee is a state of liminality, of disorder, structurelessness, and status reversal. The percentage of the world's population that are refugees is a grim fact. Worse, though, is the fact that this staggering number of refugees is created through human enterprise. Christianity's emphasis on hospitality to the stranger is of significant import for our times. It is also, as I intend to demonstrate, central to the Christian vision and to Christian discipleship.

1. Hospitality to the Stranger: Putting It in Perspective

ospitality to the stranger has to do with manifold realities that are complex and touch deep human elements. To be at home and its opposite, homelessness, touch human beings at their core. To be a stranger anywhere is never a positive characteristic. The complexity and importance of hospitality are disclosed in its etymology and history. In antiquity there is a pervasive consciousness of the singular value of hospitality toward the stranger. Such hospitality was perceived as an important sign of civilization. In fact, a mark of a lack of civilization was inhospitality toward the stranger, as often found among the "barbarians." Civilization took a decisive turn when the stranger, perceived as enemy, became a guest, one who is entertained at another's house at another's table. Such a decisive turn brought about a human community.

In ancient Greece hospitality is acknowledged and celebrated, and the lack of it decried. Homer and Plato underline many important characteristics of a civilization where hospitality toward the stranger is recognized and valued. To host a stranger does not mean simply to provide material goods but to honor the other's humanness and personhood. Also, to provide hospitality is a source of happiness and blessings. This leads some of the Greek authors to underline the fact that there seems to be a link, although mysterious, between the stranger and divinity. In fact, to be inhospitable toward the stranger is perceived as sacrilegious. Homer in *The Odyssey* affirms the following:

> Rudeness to a stranger is not decency, poor though he may be, poorer than you. All wanderers and beggars came from Zeus. What we can give is slight but the recompense great.[1]

5

In Stoic teaching there is an understanding that the relation between divinity and humanity comes from the fact that all are citizens of the same world. No one is a stranger anywhere in the world. Hospitality is foremost a great human reality—the ancients saw in hospitality to the stranger the basic characteristic of a civilized people. In classical Greek culture a stranger has to be received with hospitality, limited but well defined. "The city which forgets how to care for the stranger has forgotten how to care for itself."[2] There is a long tradition coming from the ancient Greek and Near Eastern peoples suggesting a covenant between guests and hosts. Here hospitality is perceived as fundamental to the process of humanization and as a foundation of morality. Hospitality is essential for the maintenance of order in the world; the breakdown in hospitality can only lead to a breakdown in order. Greece prides itself on hospitality to strangers. Greek religions offer Zeus's protection to strangers. Politically and legally the stranger's rights are gradually defined.

Yet hospitality is founded upon ambivalence, an ambivalence evident in the etymology of the word. In Greek, words of the *xen* stem mean "foreign" or "strange" but also "guest." For example, the verb *xenizo* means "to surprise," "to be strange," but also "to entertain." In Latin, the word that signifies host is *hospes* and the word for enemy is *hostis,* from which our word *hostile* derives. Etymologically, the word for stranger may have a negative meaning leading to xenophobia, or a positive meaning when the stranger is given hospitality, philoxenia, the love of the host.

Strangeness brings about tension between those who perceive themselves as natives, or insiders, and foreigners as outsiders. Hospitality is a way of overcoming the tension and making of the alien a friend. When a person, an outsider, is invited to a feast or to lodge with the host, that individual temporarily undergoes a change from stranger, someone who is not yet known and possibly dangerous, to guest. While the offering of hospitality does not eliminate conflict, it places such a conflict in abeyance. The relation of guest to host and host to guest is regulated by a specific code. A person who is a guest in the host's home for the first time is given precedence over habitual guests. In antiquity the stranger—

that is, the one who does not belong to one's clan, one's race, one's family, or one's religion—can be considered in two different ways: as enemy or as host. Hospitality has to do with treating the stranger as host.

A stranger can be defined for our purpose as someone who seeks to be accepted or tolerated by an individual or a group that he or she approaches. Examples for such a situation can be that of an immigrant, of a minority; strangeness can be brought about by race, gender, religion. The stranger is the one who does not share the "world," the cultural patterns, of the one who is being approached. The stranger is the one who has to place in question nearly everything that is questionable to the host. The stranger is vulnerable. Strangers find themselves in an unfamiliar world, one differently organized than that from which they come—full of pitfalls and hard to master. Approaching strangers have to anticipate what they will find.

To the stranger the cultural pattern of the approached group does not have the authority of tested values. There is no sharing of a tradition, of a history, of narratives. The stranger is a newcomer, vulnerable, an outsider and at times a marginal figure. The stranger is the one on the verge of two different cultures, not knowing where he or she belongs. The stranger is in a state of transition in a different land. Often the stranger has lost his or her bearings. The stranger is homeless.

Home

The force of hospitality to the stranger cannot be understood without grasping the meaning of homelessness, and homelessness cannot be fully understood without knowing what home means. The word *home* derives from the stem *kei,* which has a variety of meanings. Home is a safe place; it is an affective place. It is a community in which communion should exist; it is habitable. Home is settled existence. The Greek word *oikos,* "home," expresses one of the most fundamental social, economic, political, and personal realities of the ancient world. It describes house as home, the place where I belong, where I have rights and obligations. The verb *oiken* means "to inhabit, permanently reside," in our own contemporary sense, to be "at home." There are connotations of familiarity, of personal and interpersonal space. The adjective *oikeios* denotes domestic issues and affairs. Home as place has its own energy. Mary Douglas sees home as an instrument for structuring collective effort toward a moral community. Home has the ability to "muster solidarity and demand sacrifice."[3]

In his essay "The Homecomer" social theorist Alfred Schutz has reflected on the profound meaning of home. Home is central to the human experience because it has to do not simply with a place but with a state of being. Issues of identity, belonging, and origin have to do with home. "Geographically 'home' means a certain spot on the surface of the earth. Where I happen to be is my 'abode'; where I intend to stay is my 'residence'; where I come from and whither I want to return is my 'home.'"[4] When the extraterrestrial creature in Spielberg's *E.T.* points to the heavens and moans "home," the audience resonates with the drama.

The term *home* refers to affective elements. Less simply a space than a place of intensity, of emotional energy, "home is where the heart is." For example, the statement "I'm going home" does not principally express the intention to return to the building in which one lives but to a very special world within the world. The home, by providing a locale for food preparation and sleep, brings to the fore the biorhythms of everyday life.

The symbolic character of the notion of home is complex. It can and does mean different things for different people. It can mean that which is missed: a father, a mother, a spouse, or ice-cold milk. Home will mean something different for the one who never has left it and the one who lives far from it. Again, to be "at home" implies familiarity, mutuality, respect, security. It means that communication with another and understanding of the other can follow established patterns. In the home reality is predictable; the "other" is not an abstraction.

It is a constant tendency for humanity to define its dwelling place through boundaries. So there is built in the notion of home, an inside and an outside. Within our boundaries there can be domestic peace; outside, life can be dangerous and hostile. At the same time that the inside offers comfort, it also offers a chance to communicate with "neighbors" and their living spaces. Boundaries of human living need not be exclusive. As Jürgen Moltmann affirms, "The possessions of one's own living space and community with other living things in a shared living space are not mutually exclusive; they condition one another mutually."[5] A home is a place of experiences. Homes capture experience and store it symbolically. Homes are platforms for visions and plans about the future. As places of experience, they provide us with identity to venture out into less orderly places.

For Walter Brueggemann, home is not simply a space but a place.

> Place is space which has historic meanings, where some things have happened which are now remembered and which provide continuity and identity across generations. Place is space in which important words have been spoken which have established identity, defined vocation, and envisioned destiny.... Place...is a declaration that our humanness cannot be found in escape, detachment, absence of commitment, and undefined freedom.[6]

For Gaston Bachelard, "House is one of the greatest powers of integration for the thoughts, the memories and dreams of mankind."[7] For Katherine Platt, "Homes are contexts in which the self is accounted for in many concrete ways and the boundaries and curtains of the self can be drawn."[8]

James Duncan perceives the home as a symbol of the social structure.

> The built environment, in addition to providing shelter, serves as a medium of communication because encoded within it are elements of the social structure. It speaks in the language of objects about the moral order of that culture. It serves as the stage set for the morality play, the backdrop for that collection of stories that a people tell themselves about themselves, in order that they may better know who they are, how to behave and what to cherish.[9]

Home is where one starts from and one intends to return. To leave home is to enter into another social structure, into another world. The familiar no longer exists. What one has are memories.

In a more radical form, one can experience nostalgia: the pain of being away. Leaving home clearly involves a loss and a form of bereavement. Witness the French expression "Partir est mourir un peu." (To leave is to die a little.) Sometimes such a loss involves growth and development. In other situations, when leaving home is a forced process, the loss takes on a different character: a loss of roots, of a sense of history, of a sense of place. It is from this concept of home that one can understand what homelessness is and what hospitality means.

The image of home assures me of who I am and gives me a specific value. Homelessness is spiritually, personally, economically traumatic; homeless people are perceived as a threat because home-owners fear their desperate situation. According to Rosemary Haughton, "That is also why homelessness is so spiritually as well as economically traumatic, and why homeless people are often objects of fear and suspicion. They don't fit in and their 'not belonging' is a threat to the sense of stability everyone wants. It could happen to us; perhaps if we can blame them and remove them we shall feel more secure."[10]

The universal recognition of the *oikos* as the basis for human existence accounts for the trauma of its felt absence. The psychological and spiritual significance also accounts for the importance of hospitality to the stranger. As Haughton writes:

> It is this emotional power in the idea and experience of home that makes hospitality so significant as a solvent of social and moral dualisms. The history of humankind is horribly also the history of the lengths to which groups of people will go to protect the bit of ground they call home, or to regain it if it has been conquered. Yet also history is about the settling of refugees in another land, about emigration and immigration, about how aliens become inhabitants, able to claim ownership and often, in their turn, to resist and denounce new immigrants. When nations, as well as individual homeowners, practice hospitality, they take great credit for it and also surround it with safeguards, as I have suggested, and they do this because home is about identity. Home is the place where I belong, and that belongs to me. It defines who I am. The image of home, the symbols and festivals and memories, assure me of who I am and give me a specific value. Even the travelers' wagons and the

tents of nomads are home; they define the people and the culture—
and are often perceived as a threat to the settled people who claim, or
want to claim, ownership of the places where the wanderers travel.[11]

Hospitality

Hospitality is built into the reality of home. Hospitality is made
possible by the having of a home. Home is that which is available
for hospitality. The ability to welcome others into one's home
ensures that home remains home and does not become isolation,
a fortress, one's impregnable fortress. Far from being dissolved by
hospitality, home becomes quite different and yet more what it
should really be. Hospitality gives a meaning to home founded on
our common humanness, on the bonds of responsibility
anchored in our social nature. Rosemary Haughton writes, "Without ownership there cannot be hospitality; but ownership
becomes something different—legally, emotionally, morally —
when it is governed by a question: ownership for what? And the
answer is itself hospitality, of space, of ideas, of creativity."[12]

The word *hospitality,* taken in a broad sense, expresses the
willingness to share not only our possessions but that which, in
some sense, is ours in a private and personal sense, our home.
So hospitality is always a breaking down of barriers, of boundaries, of one's space. Ancient rituals and symbols regulate the
practice of hospitality. It is not surprising that in an ordinary
way and in an ordinary world hospitality is offered to chosen
friends. In emphasizing this aspect of hospitality, one loses the
sense of hospitality as the bond between strangers. As Henri
Nouwen affirms, "The paradox of hospitality is that it wants to
create an emptiness, not a fearful emptiness, but a friendly
emptiness where strangers can enter and discover themselves
as created free; free to sing their own songs, speak their own
languages, dance their own dances; free also to leave and follow
their own vocations. Hospitality is not a subtle invitation to
adopt the lifestyle of the host, but the gift of a chance for the
guest to find his own."[13]

Hospitality involves the acceptance of the "other" as other. According to Parker Palmer, hospitality "means valuing the strangeness of the stranger.... It means meeting the stranger's needs while allowing him or her simply to be, without attempting to make the stranger over into a modified version of ourselves."[14]

The stranger is in the public realm. In some real way, we are all strangers; strangeness is universal. "Do not oppress the stranger," for we are strangers. The means of hospitality lie in the private realm. Hospitality means inviting the stranger into our private space, whether that be the space of our own home or the space of our personal awareness and concern. When hospitality happens, private places are transformed and also our own private selves. According to the Judeo-Christian vision, God is encountered in a new way in the gift of hospitality. As Palmer states, "Through the stranger our view of self, of world, of God is deepened and expanded. Through the stranger we are given a chance to find ourselves. And through the stranger, God finds us and offers us the gift of wholeness in the midst of our estranged lives, a gift of God and of the public life."[15]

Hospitality performs a transformation of the way one thinks. Hospitality questions one's ways of thinking about oneself and the other as belonging to different spheres; it breaks down categories that isolate. Hospitality involves a way of thinking without the presumption of knowing beforehand what is in the mind of the other; dialogue with the other is essential. I must let the other tell me who he or she is. Hospitality decenters our perspective; my story counts but so does the story of the other. In hospitality, the stranger comes vulnerable, not at home, often in need of sustenance and shelter. To welcome the other means the willingness to enter the world of the other, to let the other tell his or her story. So listening becomes a basic attitude of hospitality. Being hospitable means being genuinely open to the other, interested in sharing, learning, and receptive to the learning the other might possess. Hospitality provides an occasion to discover something new; for example, the disciples of Emmaus finally getting to truly recognize who Jesus is.

Hospitality, by demanding on our part an attentive listening to the other, presupposes the ability to perceive the other as an equal. There is a sharing of a common humanity, of blessings and sufferings. To welcome the other into our own world implies our willingness to enter the other's world. The other's world is valued. Hospitality has to do with breaking down barriers. As Rosemary Haughton writes, "To invite another person into the space I regard as my own is, at least temporarily, to give up a measure of privacy. It is already to make a breach in the division between the public and the private to create the common—and it happens in the space called home."[16]

One's capacity for hospitality is always precarious, tenuous, difficult, for it has to do with home, privacy. Home is space protected, restricted; hospitality transforms such a space. In hospitality host and guest enter into a partnership where each accepts responsibility for the other's well-being. Different periods in history, different cultures have facilitated hospitality and "partnership with strangers." Our times and culture are marked by a deep ambiguity, by fear and distrust of the stranger. Such a culture will not facilitate the Judeo-Christian vision of hospitality to the stranger. The lack of hospitality is a sure sign of our lack of civilization. The absence of hospitality in our churches is a sure mark of their inauthenticity. "He came to what was his own, and his own people did not accept him" (John 1:11).

2. Hospitality to the Stranger in America

According to David Hollenbach, a renewed American commitment to the common good is crucial to our contemporary American society. The author refers to Aristotle and Aquinas, "Over two millennia ago Aristotle argued that the good of the community should set the direction for the lives of individuals for it is a higher or more 'divine' good than the particular goods of private persons."[1] In a Christian context, St. Thomas argued that a right relation to God requires commitment to the common good of our neighbors and creation. It is exactly our attitude toward the common good that is most indicative of where our contemporary culture lies. Concern for the common good is an essential element of our nature as public and social beings. Our depreciation of the public dimension of our human reality is enormously detrimental. As Parker Palmer writes, "We lose our sense of relatedness to those strangers with whom we must share the earth, we lose our sense of comfort and at-homeness in the world."[2]

Hollenbach reminds us that "for Christians, the pursuit of the common good follows from the Bible's double commandment to love God with all one's heart and to love one's neighbor as oneself."[3] The double commandment, crucial for the survival of concern for the common good, is equally crucial for the existence and valuation of another Christian "commandment"—to be hospitable to the stranger.

While Jesus' invitation to love God and love our neighbor, even our enemy, has become an intrinsic part of Christianity's self-understanding, translating this invitation in practice has proven to be difficult. The Last Judgment scene in Matthew (25:31–46) announces the difficulty of connecting love of God with love of the stranger. Love of God is problematic in itself; to affirm that

God loves us is equally problematic. To love our enemy is not something into which we easily fall.

Hospitality to the stranger, while not necessarily yet love, is, in Christianity, perceived to be anchored in the love of God. Like love, hospitality to the stranger is problematic. While human sinfulness is clearly one of the factors, so is our contemporary culture. The biblical invitation to be hospitable to the stranger is in serious trouble in our culture today.

The idea that we should use our freedom to nurture the common good rather than to seek our own pleasures has long been at the center of Christian and Jewish ethics. Yet it has always been fragile; if not carefully nurtured, it will certainly die. To nurture concern for the common good it is necessary once again to remember the commandment to love God and neighbor. The ethic of neighbor-love calls for sacrifice for the stranger. Neighbor is the "other," not simply the one who lives near us in a geographical sense. It is not a question of loving only those who are close to us, who think the same way we think; the command of love is universal. Hospitality in the Christian sense is counter-cultural; it is based on the capability that love has to constitute its object of love. Such love is symbolic of God's love for creation. The command to love our neighbors does not demand feelings of emotional intimacy for everyone; what is required is to act with love toward the "other" simply because the other is God's creature and as such a presence of God. According to Stephen Carter:

> To enter into the presence of another human being, then, is to enter into the presence of God in a new and different way. We are admonished in the psalm to come into His presence with thanksgiving (Ps 95:2), not with suspicion, self-seeking, or disrespect. The great theologians Karl Barth and Martin Buber both arrived at this point along their different paths: our obligation is to see God in everyone, not merely as possibility, but as reality. So whenever we mistreat others, we are abusing our relationship with God. And awe alone does not capture what we owe. We should encounter others with a sense of gratitude, for here is a fresh and different corner of God's creation — or, for the secular-minded, a new and different human being. We should be grateful to be traveling where we have not been before.[4]

Hospitality to the stranger entails more than almsgiving. According again to Carter, it involves "an orientation of the soul, toward the other, the one who is outside of us and may seem very different from us, and yet is part of us through our equal share in God's creation."[5]

Unfortunately, our contemporary culture is not conducive to the realization of the scriptural command to be hospitable to the stranger. This is clearly evident in the plight of the refugees and homeless. There are countless conditions of rootlessness, marginality, and homelessness in the modern world. More than a decade ago, celebrities and citizens joined in high-profile efforts like Hands Across America, which raised awareness and 15 million dollars for the cause. Now the issue is back in a big way, only instead of sympathy, the homeless are attracting hostility. According to a report by the National Law Center on Homelessness and Poverty, at least twenty-four cities have used police to forcibly remove the homeless from certain sections of town. While so many other social ills seem to be on the mend, the homeless situation remains as bad or worse. What has changed is the tolerance level. Anti-vagrancy laws, which are anti-homeless laws, suggest that middle-class Americans have exhausted their reserves of compassion for the homeless and now see them as responsible for their own destiny.

Ebbing Concern for the Stranger

In our culture today concern for the stranger seems to be ebbing. Strangers such as refugees or the homeless are perceived as constituting threats to our sense of home, to our ability to earn a good living, to our possessions. Yet it seems unnatural for Americans to kick people when they are down. For example, the Illegal Immigration and Immigrant Responsibility Act of 1996 is characterized by meanness and has caused untold hardship. These laws seem to have taken away from Americans the right to be compassionate. This is not only un-American, it is clearly against Judeo-Christian beliefs: "For if you...do not oppress the alien...then I will dwell with you in this place...that I gave of old to your ancestors forever and ever" (Jer 7:5-7).

One needs to ask what has happened in our culture to lead us to such an atmosphere. While the answer is complex, it has to do in part with a centrifugal force at work in contemporary society: individualism.[6] Our culture is the most individualist in human history. It is focused on personal choice rather than concern for the common good. People "do their own thing"—except for those who lack the means and the powers to do just that.

Individualism is defined as making self-interest the criterion for determining what is good, true, valuable, and moral. Individualism has eclipsed communal structures and meaning. According to Mark Searle and his colleagues, rugged Americans influenced not only our social fabric but our religious identity as well. In his summary of the results of a Notre Dame study, Searle highlighted Robert Bellah's conclusions by noting that

> there is strong evidence that *American Catholics are in the process of becoming more characteristically American than characteristically Catholic. In other words, cultural assimilation appears to be occurring at the expense of a distinctive Catholic identity.* In their moral, political, and social attitudes, Catholics are becoming indistinguishable from the rest of the population. *Where liturgy is concerned, this means a growing alienation from precisely that sense of collective identity and collective responsibility which the liturgy might be thought to rehearse.* It is a threat to the integrity of the liturgical act. Far from being able to inure Catholics against the negative aspects of their wider culture, the liturgy may actually be succumbing to such influences.[7]

If what Bellah and Searle report is true, this cultural assimilation implies that personal values of self-interest are replacing communal values, and that the individual is given priority over the community. Communal values as articulated in public worship are instrumental in bringing about political and social participation; their absence is detrimental to any society.

Christopher Lasch writes, "Every society reproduces its culture—its norms, its underlying assumptions, its modes of organizing experience—in the individual, in the form of personality."[8] Technological culture has given rise to the narcissistic personality. Narcissism has been recognized as an important element in contemporary character disorders. So the age of technology has developed its own peculiar form of pathology. Lasch writes, "Modern capitalist society not only elevates narcissists to prominence, it elicits and reinforces narcissistic traits in everyone."[9]

Social Sciences and Selfishness

Narcissism, as Lasch recognizes, is not simply cultural.[10] Ernest Becker claims that narcissism is inescapable, because it has a biological basis in human nature.[11] The human organism has an inherent tendency to incorporate and expand and protect itself against the world. Sociobiology does not suggest that we are genetically selfish. The sociobiologists attest that we are genetically predisposed to be kind to people in proportion to how closely related to us they are. In biology, altruism exists solely as a factor for reproductive success. The crux of evolution is not the good of the species but the good of the individual gene. Richard Dawkins writes, "The predominant quality to be expected in a successful gene is ruthless selfishness. This gene selfishness will usually give rise to selfishness in individual behavior."[12] The author warns his readers that in the building of a society

> in which individuals cooperate generously and unselfishly toward a common good, you can expect little help from biological nature. Let us try to teach generosity and altruism, because we are born selfish. Let us understand what our own selfish genes are up to, because we may then at least have the chance to upset their designs, something which no other species has ever aspired to.[13]

Sociobiology suggests that much of our behavior has a calculated, selfish, deceitful quality. Elaborate religious, social, and linguistic networks are erected to mark underlying manipulative motivations.

The dominant modern psychologies explain human behavior in terms of individual pleasure and pain, individual positive and negative valence, individual needs and drives.[14] In social psychology social interaction is analyzed exclusively in terms of the self. Psychologists and psychiatrists almost invariably side with self-gratification over traditional restraint.[15] Phillip Rieff underlines the

18

fact that contemporary culture proposes an ethic of self-realization for which the well-being of the individual is of the highest value.[16]

Many Western philosophies have seen the "other" not in its full otherness but as an occasion for self-discovery or self-realization. The other is accounted for as a valuable investment, which will pay off eventually in the dividend of one's own self-realization. Erich Fromm, who has emphasized the importance of the other, still defines the relation between self and other in terms of self-realization. For him, the goal is "any aim which furthers the growth, freedom and happiness of the self." He writes:

> The character structure of the mature and integrated personality, the productive character, constitutes the source and the basis of virtue.... "Vice," in the last analysis, is indifference to one's own self and self-mutilation. Not self-renunciation nor selfishness but self-love, not the negation of the individual but the affirmation of his truly human self, are the supreme values of humanistic ethics. If man is to have confidence in values, he must know himself and the capacity of his nature for goodness and productiveness.[17]

Fromm makes self-realization the end purpose of any growth, and relation to others simply the means to that end.

The social sciences not only describe people as selfishly motivated but teach that they ought to be so. Sociobiology holds repression and inhibition of individual impulse to be undesirable; it considers all guilt to be dysfunctional neurosis created by cruel child rearing and a repressive society. The contemporary climate is therapeutic. People identify personal salvation with the feeling of personal well-being, health, and the psychic security they crave. In this context love and meaning are defined as the fulfillment of the patient's emotional appetites. The self-sacrifice and self-abasement of the old concept of love are seen as oppressive—offensive to common sense and bad for one's health. The liberation of humanity from such outdated ideas as love and duty has become the mission of the converts and popularizers of the post-Freudian therapies, for whom mental health means the overthrow of inhibitions and the resultant elevation of self: individuality over community, the elevation of the self, and the desires of the self above all else. The call for hospitality to the stranger provides the necessary way to resist the fragmentation of an excessive individualism. Hospitality given or received in our hardened and bottom-line world may often be experienced as gracious mystery.

It is not surprising, then, that a retreat to purely personal satisfaction is one of the main themes of our culture. There has been yet another revival of the cults of expanded consciousness, health, and personal growth. To live for oneself in the moment is the prevailing code. Survival has become the catchword of today and a resentful, attenuated narcissism the dominant disposition.[18] What is being cultivated is a transcendental self-attention. Emphasis on the individual is detrimental to any sustained concern for the common good, any effort to build community. A narcissistic society is also a consumerist society.

Consumerism and Individualism

In a consumerist society the mere accumulation of goods and services is perceived as enough for the realization of human happiness. We are only as we possess. To nurture and sustain itself, a consumer culture relies on various structural elements, basically those of a capitalist society. In such a society the communal is displaced to the level of personal reality, and the individual is made solely responsible for doing something about it. Consumerism reinforces excessive individualism. An increase in material consumption does not necessarily result in an increase in well-being. The principle of unlimited consumption as the goal of life can lead only to disharmony. In a limited world, unlimited consumption implies the deprivation of some through the unlimited egotism of others.

Under the strain of radical individualism and factionalism, the civic life of the country deteriorates. America grows increasingly coarse and uncivil. Incivility creates and exacerbates distance between people. People then withdraw into self-selective mirrored chambers where "otherness" and strangeness are excluded. Rights are everywhere demanded. For many, individual civil liberties stand immovable as an absolute value: rights of privacy, freedom of expression, freedom of action, freedom to acquire, freedom to indulge any whim whatsoever. Rights without responsibilities can lead only to radical factionalism.

Radical individualism can lead only to an extreme xenophobia. If friendly feelings are intrinsic to human beings, unfriendly ones certainly are as well. Many, in fact, believe that unfriendly feelings are *more* intrinsic since a case can be made that evolutionary survival depends not on cooperation but on superiority of various kinds. The seriousness of xenophobia in our time can scarcely be overstated.

Reflecting on the meaning of land and place in the Hebrew scriptures, Walter Brueggemann writes:

> The sense of being lost, displaced, and homeless is pervasive in contemporary culture. The yearning to belong somewhere, to have a home, to be in a safe place, is a deep and moving pursuit. Loss of place and yearning for place are dominant images. They may be understood in terms of sociological displacement, as Americans have become a *"nation of strangers,"* highly mobile and rootless, as our entire social fabric becomes an artifact designed for obsolescence, and the design includes even us consumers! They may be understood in terms of psychological dislocation, as increasing numbers of persons are disoriented, characterized as possessors of "the homeless mind." The despair and yearning are expressed in the pathos of the "top forty" songs among the young, in the fear among the old that they are forgotten, in the helplessness of the poor in the face of "urban progress." Remarkably the same sense of loss and the same yearning for place are much in evidence among those whom the world perceives as being well rooted and belonging, the white middle class at the peak of success and productivity. Those whom we imagine to be secure and invested with "turf" in our time experience profound dislocation, and we are, young and old, rich and poor, black and white, "as having everything, and yet possessing nothing" (cf. 2 Cor 6:10).[19]

Hospitality to the stranger demands sacrifice: to surrender our biases; to make the interests, joys, and sorrows of others our own. As such, hospitality to the stranger is subversive by nature, threatening to the existing powers. Such subversive power is most needed in a culture that encourages space over place.

3. The Foundations of Hospitality to the Stranger

mphasis on hospitality to the stranger has its foundation in both scriptures: the Jewish and the Christian. There are many texts in the Hebrew Bible that make clear that hospitality to the stranger is God's wish. Two Hebrew terms express two different ways of being a stranger. *Nokri,* or *Ben-Nekar,* designates one who is a stranger to the religion of Israel (Exod 12:43) or the people of Israel (Deut 15:3). The other word, *Ger,* originally means one who lives outside of his/her place of origin (family, house, tribe, or country) and who therefore is a wanderer, a refugee, a host as Moses is in the country of Midian. Moses called his son Gershom because "I have been an alien residing in a foreign land" (Exod 2:22). This same term will later be used to designate all non-Israelites living in Israel. In the Septuaginta, the Hebrew words for stranger are translated by the Greek *paroikos.* This word designates the situation of living abroad as resident aliens.

In Israel the commandment to be hospitable is grounded in the remembering of the Israelite's own situation when in Egypt. "The alien who resides with you shall be to you as the citizen among you; you shall love the alien as yourself, for you were aliens in the land of Egypt" (Lev 19:34). In another text: "You shall also love the stranger, for you were strangers in the land of Egypt" (Deut 10:19).

If Israel is to be hospitable, it has to do with avoiding what happened to the Egyptians. Also it is in order to imitate God, "who is not partial and takes no bribe, who executes justice for the orphan and the widow, and who loves the strangers, providing them food and clothing" (Deut 10:17–18, cf. Ps 146:9).

The Law and Hospitality

Numerous texts in the Law make this commandment concrete through specific stipulations. The stranger will not work on the Sabbath day in order to rest (Exod 23:12; Deut 5:12-15); not everything in the field will be picked up. "When you reap your harvest in your field and forget a sheaf in the field, you shall not go back to get it; it shall be left for the alien..." (Deut 24:19-22). Here in these texts the stranger is inserted in the class of poor, the widows, and the orphans (cf. Jer 7:1-7; Zech 7:10). When Job examines his life he remembers his conduct toward the stranger: "The stranger has not lodged in the street. I have opened my doors to the traveler" (Job 31:32). The Law and the prophets speak against molesting and abusing the stranger (Exod 22:20-22; Deut 24:17-18; Jer 7:6-7). "Cursed be anyone who deprives the alien, the orphan, and the widow" (Deut 27:19). It was the Egyptian crime to oppress the stranger; they were xenophobes.

Characteristic of Israel's attitude to the stranger is its hospitality. Resident aliens enjoy rights and social acceptance. This is explicit in the following texts: "You shall support them; they shall live with you as though resident aliens....You shall not make them serve as slaves. They shall remain with you as hired or bound laborers" (Lev 25:35, 39-40a). "You shall not abhor any of the Egyptians, because you were an alien residing in their land" (Deut 23:7).

The Precariousness of the Wilderness

Remembering its existence as an alien, Israel saw its mission typified in Abraham, who accepted his alien status as a sign of faith and obedience in God. Israel is embodied in Abraham, Isaiah, and Jacob in the earlier presentations of them as sojourners on the way to a land whose name Israel does not know. The sojourn is freely chosen in faith and hope, not imposed. They choose to be sojourners, which technically means to be in a place as an outsider, never belonging. To sojourn means to be on a pilgrimage. Israel's forty years in the desert is its time of wandering (Exod 16-18). This wilderness experience for Israel is one of precariousness, of landlessness, but also of grace. The negative and

23

positive aspects of Israel's wandering are captured in the theme of wilderness. The constant need to survive and the constant absence of resources challenge faith.

Being in the wilderness is a difficult and precarious situation, especially if one feels abandoned even by God. For Israel, the questions became: What connection is there between wilderness and God's presence? Is the wilderness simply an in-between time? How can God be known in a period of transition? Is the wilderness a place God prefers for a special kind of presence? The wilderness poses the question of who is our God. The "desert period" is the fundamental time of Israel's encounter with and knowledge of God. It is in the desert that God reveals Godself to Moses.

Knowledge of God comes through wandering and through movement. "A wandering Aramean was my ancestor" (Deut 26:5). It is during this period that there emerges a religious tradition in which generosity and hospitality and justice are emphasized. It was in the wilderness that Israel experienced the care, guidance, and compassion of God. "He sustained him in a desert land, in a howling wilderness waste; he shielded him, cared for him, and guarded him as the apple of his eye" (Deut 32:10).

While the wilderness is a hostile place, a place of trial, it is there that God is revealed as a faithful God. "I am who am." The wilderness stories in Exodus and Numbers combine the elements of danger, threat, and grace. Like the manna from heaven, God's gracious presence is always enough for survival. It is always gift, freely given. Like the manna that cannot be stored, God can never be a house idol, never presumed upon. "He knows your going through this great wilderness. These forty years the Lord your God has been with you; you have lacked nothing" (Deut 2:7). "I have led you forty years in the wilderness. The clothes on your back have not worn out, and the sandals on your feet have not worn out" (Deut 29:5). The wilderness, which can easily be a place of death, was a place of life. Where there was nothing, where Israel should have perished, nothing was lacking. Yet Israel yearned for a land, for a homeland.

24

The meaning of home and the sense of place is a universal reality. It would be strange if this were not true for Israel. To be rooted in a place is a primary concern for Israel and a primary category of faith. Home and place for Israel are expressed in the category of land—land promised, given, lost, and recovered. Such a land is a place with Yahweh. Israel's entire history is marked by a hope for land and a response to the gift of land. *Oikos* and its Hebrew equivalent, *Bayith*, express communal identity and relate to issues of political and religious solidarity. The covenant established by God in its particular dimension is with the household of Israel, the house of Jacob, the house of Israel. The Israelite community is defined in terms of home. God is the master builder of the house of Israel, the giver of the land; the greatest tragedy that can affect Israel is the loss of land, dissolution of the household of God.

Land means having roots, belonging, stability, possession. Land is a reality and a symbol. The symbolic sense of land affirms that land is never simply physical ground but ground with meaning and history. There is a surplus of meaning to land known only to those who lose and yearn for it. The Hebrew scriptures address the issue of homelessness in terms of land given, possessed, and lost. For Abraham, to accept landlessness is a posture of faith; for Israel, to accept land demands a posture of gratitude, responsibility, and hospitality. "Land with God brings responsibility. The same land which is gift freely given is task sharply put."[1] As gift, land is made to be shared with others. Greed for land, grasping the land "leads to homelessness."[2] Walter Brueggemann states a basic dialectic concerning land in Israel: "The first is a history of risking homelessness which yields the gift of home. The second is the deep yearning for home, but in ways which result in homelessness."[3] Brueggemann sees a third history, that of Jesus: "And in the third history, from exile to Jesus, we learn that Jesus' embrace of homelessness (crucifixion) is finally the awesome, amazing gift of home (resurrection)."[4]

There are implications for the fact that the land which the Israelites occupied was a gift of God, for it was a gift given to all people. "The land shall not be sold in perpetuity, for the land is mine; with me you are but aliens and tenants. Throughout the land you hold, you shall provide for the redemption of the land" (Lev 25:23 -24). There can be no ultimate claim to the land. Yet with possession of land also comes the possibility of dispossession. Laws are directed toward helping the dispossessed. The people are to care for the sojourners, because they themselves were once sojourners. "You shall also love the stranger, for you were strangers in the land of Egypt" (Deut 10:19). All are equal before God for "the land is mine; for you are all strangers and sojourners with me" (Lev 25:23).

Israel and the sojourners are equal before God; everything is from God. They are under the same law (Lev 24:22). From the perspective of the covenanted land emerges this mandate: "I therefore command you, 'Open your hand to the poor and needy neighbor in your land'" (Deut 15:11). Israel is to care for the stranger because Israel was once a sojourner. Possession of the land, which relieves Israel from the status of sojourner, is only because of God's redeeming grace. Oppression of the stranger, of the poor, is an act against the covenant. As Luke Johnson writes:

> When God called Israel into being as a people, he redeemed those who were themselves oppressed (Exod 2:23 -25; 3:7 -10). His power to "work justice" for the oppressed has not ceased. Those who oppress the poor will have to deal with God's avenging anger. If the poor, the widows, or the oppressed cry out to God, he will hear them and punish the oppressor (Exod 22:21 -27; Deut 25:9). Those who pervert justice by taking bribes will have to deal with "the great, the mighty, and the terrible" God, who is not partial and takes no bribe. He executes justice for the fatherless and the widow, and loves the sojourner, giving him food and clothing (Deut 10:17 -18).[5]

Justice toward the stranger, toward the poor, is demanded by God's covenantal relationship. "I am the Lord your God, who brought you out of the land of Egypt. You shall keep all my statutes and all my ordinances, and observe them: I am the Lord" (Lev 19:36 -37). The same covenantal motivation for justice marks the prophets' attacks against those who oppress and who pervert justice. "Render true judgments; show kindness and mercy each to one another, do not oppress the widow, the orphan, the alien, or the poor; and do not devise evil in your hearts against one another" (Zech 7:9-10). The condemnation of oppression of the stranger has to do with the breaking of the covenant with God. Israel's response to the poor, the stranger, articulates its response to God.

Land in Israel is connected to wealth and possession. Possession and wealth often lead to oppression of the poor, of the alien. The prophets constantly oppose those who live in luxury and oppress the poor (Amos 6:1). The punishment for such oppression is the loss of possession (Hos 9:6).

Landlessness and dispossession for Israel is the Exile. Exile is the lowest point for Israel, homelessness in its worst aspects. Such homelessness came to pass in the days of Jeremiah, who announced its coming. It is also the collapse of the household of God. "I have forsaken my house; I have abandoned my heritage" (Jer 12:7). God is the master builder of the house of Israel; the greatest ill that can affect Israel is the dissolution of the household of God. Dislocation from home and dispossession of the land, like the wilderness, were the experiences that shaped the language and symbolism of religious despair and hope. Like in the wilderness, the Exile becomes for Israel a time of faith and hope. It is a time for yearning, for newness (Jer 31:17-18). In the context of the Exile, the promises loom larger.

Land is always a problem in Israel, and so "Israel is always on the move from land to landlessness, from landlessness to land, from life to death, from death to life. It's historical character derives from its questing for promises seemingly so rich and fulsome, but so burdened with ambiguity and loss."[6] For Israel, the land is to be given to those who are vulnerable and see themselves as not having any right to expect it. Land is a gift. "The land to Israel is a gift from Yahweh and binds Israel in new ways to the giver."[7] As God's gift, land is a sacrament of God's promise and word.

As a gift, the land given to Israel does not come from coercion. "For the land that you are about to enter to occupy is not like the land of Egypt, from which you have come, where you sow your seed and irrigate by foot, like a vegetable garden. But the land that you are crossing over to occupy is a land of hills and valleys, watered by rain from the sky, a land that the Lord your God looks after. The eyes of the Lord your God are always on it, from the beginning of the year to the end of the year" (Deut 11:10–12). So Israel's land always implies involvement with God—no land without God, no God without land. The two are held together.

Israel's land is covenanted land; the place it offers is covenanted place. Uncovenanted land in Israel is dangerous—and destructive. The gift of land comes with a warning: "Take care that you do not forget the Lord, who brought you out of the land of Egypt, out of the house of slavery" (Deut 6:12). "Take care that you do not forget the Lord your God by failing to keep his commandments and his ordinances, and his statutes.... Do not exalt yourself, forgetting the Lord your God, who brought you out of the land of Egypt, out of the house of slavery, who led you through the great and terrible wilderness...and fed you in the wilderness with manna.... Do not say to yourself, 'My power and the might of my own hand have gotten me this wealth'" (Deut 8:11–17). "Take care, or you will be seduced into turning away" (Deut 11:16). The nonnegotiable character of Israel's land is that it is received; it is given "to the radically undeserving."[8] "Yahweh is the Lord of *gifted existence,* taken freely and without merit. And the way to sustain gifted existence is to stay singularly with the gift-giver."[9]

Yet the land contains in itself temptations toward self-reliance and self-satisfaction. "That is the central temptation of the land, that it seems to contain in its own gifts adequate means to secure existence."[10] Israel can lose the land, and that is its ultimate contingency. Contingency is what Israel experienced in the wilderness. Israel's laws concerning possession are articulations of covenantal obligations toward God and toward one another. The laws against oppression emerge from the covenantal relation to the one God; oppression of the poor is truly apostasy from God, idolatry (Exod 20:1–9). Israel's response to the "other" is also a response to God. Hospitality to the stranger symbolizes Israel's response to God.

The Scriptures and Hospitality

In the Jewish scriptures hospitality always has to do with God. Now the primitive condition of the stranger is described to us in

28

chapter 4 of Genesis: "Cain said to the LORD: 'My punishment is greater than I can bear! Today you have driven me away from the soil, and I shall be hidden from your face; I shall be a fugitive and a wanderer on the earth, and anyone who meets me may kill me.' Then the LORD said to him, 'Not so! Whoever kills Cain will suffer a sevenfold vengeance.'" Far from being murdered, the stranger in Israel becomes the occasion of an encounter with God. Genesis 18 describes the mysterious depth of hospitality to the stranger. Abraham's hospitality to the three strangers is hospitality to God. Abraham hurries to find food; he kneels before his hosts, washes their feet, gives them bread and milk. These are the eternal gestures, the sacraments of hospitality. The vagrant, the wanderer, far from being despised, oppressed, murdered, becomes the occasion of an encounter with God.

The difference between the Jewish scriptures and the Christian scriptures on hospitality to the stranger is Jesus, his person and his message. "I was a stranger and you welcomed me" (Matt 25:35). Hospitality is present in much of Jesus' life and ministry. Jesus is born in a stable since there is no other place for him; Jesus is taken out of Israel into Egypt because of Herod. In his ministry Jesus is a wanderer without a home (Matt 8:20). Jesus has to accept hospitality from various individuals, such as Lazarus and his sisters. Jesus depends on hospitality (Mark 1:29ff.; 2:15ff.). "Foxes have holes, and birds of the air have nests; but the Son of Man has nowhere to lay his head" (Luke 9:58). In the Gospel of John, Jesus appears as the stranger in our midst. Hans Frei writes about Jesus the stranger: "Jesus is the archetypal man, or the pattern for authentic humanity. He is the *stranger*—as we all are—in this harsh and hostile universe.... In just this wandering estrangement, Jesus is our embodiment or representative.... In Jesus, the typical human situation finds its most early progenitor to establish his identity on earth. As early as the moment of his conception and birth, it is symbolically the case that he has no place to lay his head."[11] Christ comes into a hostile world as a stranger (Mark 12:1ff.; John 8:14, 25ff.). Even his disciples do not really know him (John 21:12) and constantly misunderstand him (John 3:4).

As mentioned earlier, *paroikos* is the word the Septuaginta chose to translate the Hebrew word for stranger. *Parokoi* is the word for displaced, dislocated persons. *Parokoi* are people who are not at home wherever they are. They do not share the same culture, do not have the same roots, the same religious allegiance. In the New Testament, the substantive *paroikos*, the verb *paroikeo* and the noun *paroikia* are used for stranger. The term is used in several instances to point to Israel's own history, especially to the story of Abraham. Paul recalls the *paroikia* of the patriarchs. "The God of this people Israel chose our ancestors and made the people great during their *paroikia* in the land of Egypt, and with uplifted arm he led them out of it" (Acts 13:17).

The Epistle to the Hebrews cites the example of Abraham: "By faith Abraham obeyed when he was called to set out.... By faith he stayed for a time (*paroikesen*) in the land he had been promised, as in a foreign land, living in tents as did Isaac and Jacob" (Heb 11:8–9). In these different texts the usual meaning of *paroikoi*—resident alien, one living away from home—is present.

The other word for stranger in the New Testament is *xenos*. Words of the *xen* stem can mean "foreign" or "strange," but also "guest." *Philoxenia* is the term for hospitality. In Jesus' message, love of the *xenos*, the stranger, is an essential command to love the neighbor. Not only toleration of the stranger is called for but also love of the stranger. *Philoxenia* in the New Testament suggests an intensification of hospitality. Many of the more important teachings of the New Testament are concerned with hospitality to the stranger: the story of the Last Judgment in Matthew 25; the story of the disciples of Emmaus; the parable of the Good Samaritan; some writings of Paul; and in 1 Peter. The fundamental vision of the Christian faith, that of the Kingdom of God, has to do with hospitality to the stranger. Hospitality to the stranger has a bearing on eternal destiny, for it has, as Matthew 25 affirms, a bearing on one's relationship to Christ.

In Matthew we have the parable about the Last Judgment (25:31–46) Jesus in the role of messiah king commends the righteous one for giving him food, for visiting him in prison, and for welcoming him when he appeared to them as a stranger. While the righteous do not remember such actions, Jesus assures them, "Truly I tell you, just as you did it to one of the least of those who are members of my family, you did it to me" (v. 40). These words recall similar words earlier in Matthew: "Whoever welcomes you welcomes me, and whoever welcomes me welcomes the one who sent me" (Matt 10:40, cf. John 13:20). One day the Christians who used to be strangers in this world will hear a familiar voice, that of Jesus, the stranger in our midst and now the host.

In various encounters with strangers, as described in the scriptures, such as the story of the disciples of Emmaus, there is a dialectic relative to the roles of guest and host: a reversal takes place. Such a dialectic is already present in the etymology of the Greek word *xenos,* which simultaneously denotes a guest, a host, or a stranger. The verb *xenizein* means "receive as a guest," but also "surprise," and hence "present someone or something as strange." In the same way, the term *philoxenia,* which is the term in the New Testament for hospitality, implies that both hosts and guest gain in their encounter. For part of the hospitable act is the presupposition that God, Christ, and the Holy Spirit, are present and involved (cf. 1 Pet 4:9-10). In the story of the stranger on the road to Emmaus (Luke 24:13-35), there is a reversal of the roles of host and guest. The disciples' hospitality to the stranger leads to the stranger's hospitality toward them. In the breaking of the bread Jesus becomes the host, and a revelation occurs: the disciples finally recognize him.

In the Gospel of Luke Jesus is presented as a wanderer without a home and in need of hospitality, yet Jesus is also the supreme host, welcoming strangers to the Kingdom of God. As if to summarize the ministry of Jesus, Luke reports: "Now all the tax collectors and sinners were coming near to listen to him. And the Pharisees and scribes were grumbling and saying, 'This fellow welcomes sinners and eats with them'" (15:1-2). "The marginal messiah welcomes other marginal people. He is God's traveling householder *(oikodespotes),* inviting every Israelite to the banquet of the kingdom (14:16-24), but in the end admitting only those who repent (13:24-30; 23:43)."[12]

In the text from Luke, Jesus invites the outcasts of society to eat with him. Some scholars argue that Jesus' practice of eating with tax collectors and sinners was both the central feature of his ministry and its major scandal. In the synoptic gospels prominence is given to Jesus' table ministry among marginal people. "Why does he eat with tax collectors and sinners?" (Mark 2:16). Jesus sits at table in the house of a tax collector. Joachim Jeremias writes "The oriental...would immediately understand the acceptance of the outcasts into table fellowship with Jesus as an offer of salvation to guilty sinners and as the assurance of forgiveness."[13]

The shared meal was not only a social act of friendship but was also a religious act of fellowship with God. For Jesus, such an act is open to all. Jesus' table fellowship is disruptive of any form of exclusiveness. Outsiders become insiders; there is no discrimination here. What is proclaimed in Luke 4 as the heart of Jesus' ministry—good news to the poor, release to the captives, freedom for the oppressed—and what is manifested as well by his healings of the sick is pushed to an extreme in his invitation to the ritually unclean to eat with him. Such table fellowship functions as a disorienting symbol. It subverts accepted structures for behavior and ethical existence. Related to Jesus' preaching about the Kingdom of God, it indicates that the way of the Kingdom is not the way of the world. In the Kingdom of God there is no discrimination, no dualism such as rich and poor. Hospitality to the stranger epitomizes the scandal of exclusiveness. "Listen, I am standing at the door, and knocking; if you hear my voice and open the door, I will come in to you and eat with you, and you with me" (Rev 3:20).

It seems clear that Jesus' persistent attention to food, drink, and hospitality is intended to convey something important about the reciprocal relationship between God and human beings. Behind Jesus' imagery is the magnanimous God, who constantly grants far more than humans need or deserve (Matt 5:43-48).

Hospitality to the stranger is intrinsically connected both in the Jewish and Christian scriptures to issues of possessions, of riches, of poverty. The poor and the stranger are privileged in the eyes of God. When Jesus starts his ministry, he reads Isaiah 61:1-2:

32

"The Spirit of the Lord is upon me
  because he has anointed me
    to bring good news to the poor.
He has sent me to proclaim release to the captives
    and recovery of sight to the blind,
    to let the oppressed go free,
  to proclaim the year of the Lord's favor." (Luke 4:18-19)

The poor are not only those who are without possessions but those who are oppressed, those who are at the margin of society, those who are strangers and aliens in their own country. The concern for the poor is the issue in the parable given while sitting in the house of the Pharisee (Luke 14:10-24). Here the poor stand first in line, outcasts that they are. The parable serves as a model for human hospitality. "When you give a banquet, invite the poor, the crippled, the lame, and the blind. And you will be blessed, because they cannot repay you" (Luke 14:13-14).

The New Testament letter of James continues the witness of the Law to the church. James asserts clearly that the way we respond to other human beings "who are made in the likeness of God" (Jas 3:9) is the way to respond to God. Living faith in God is to be articulated and measured by response to the needs of the poor, the alien. "If a brother or sister is naked and lacks daily food, and one of you says to them, 'Go in peace; keep warm and eat your fill,' and yet you do not supply their bodily needs, what is the good of that? So faith by itself, if it has no works, is dead" (Jas 2:15-17). James is reiterating the fundamental statement of the Law and the prophets for Christian discipleship: "Religion that is pure and undefiled before God, the Father, is this: to care for orphans and widows in their distress, and to keep oneself unstained by the world" (Jas 1:27).

Both in the Hebrew and Christian scriptures hospitality to the stranger is connected to the presence of God. The author of Hebrews gives the example of Abraham to underline the importance of hospitality: "Do not neglect to show hospitality to strangers, for by doing that some have entertained angels without knowing it" (Heb 13:2). Hospitality in the scriptures is holy ground. According to Matthew and John, Jesus once told his

33

disciples, "Whoever welcomes you welcomes me, and whoever welcomes me welcomes the one who sent me" (Matt 10:40). This is illustrated in Luke's story of the disciples of Emmaus. Two disciples are journeying; they have abandoned their discipleship because of the trauma of the cross. Leaving Jerusalem is a code word for leaving discipleship. They are encountered by a stranger who appears to be unaware of the crucifixion. Cleophas, one of the two, exclaims, "Are you the only resident alien *(paroikeis)* in Jerusalem who does not know the things that have happened in these days?" (Luke 24:18). The disciples' eyes "were kept from recognizing him" (v. 16). Faith for Luke is seeing, and lack of faith is what led the two to abandon discipleship. The stranger opens their eyes so that they can grasp the meaning of God's plan as realized in the person of Jesus. It is in offering hospitality to Jesus the stranger that the two former disciples truly see. The lordship of Jesus is discovered in a meal, in an act of hospitality. Through their act of hospitality to a stranger the two hosts are transformed and renewed in their discipleship. In the New Testament the heights and depths of human reality can be revealed in the sacred bond established between guests and hosts in the act of hospitality. God's presence is to be discovered in ordinary exchanges between human guests and hosts.

Here in this story of the disciples of Emmaus a stranger is the central figure, a stranger with an important message. As Thomas Merton wrote, "No man knows that the stranger he meets...is not already an invisible member of Christ and perhaps one who has some providential or prophetic message to utter."[14] The disciples of Emmaus abandoned discipleship because they could not make any sense of the cross, of the death of Jesus as a criminal. How could God's beloved Son suffer such a death? They finally understood when the stranger not only explained the scriptures to them but broke the bread. Jesus broke bread with the outcasts and in doing so made himself an outcast. He died an outcast because he had made himself an outcast. They recognize in the breaking of the bread the stranger who now functions as their host.

Hospitality has to do with the bringing about of a commitment between guests and hosts. The relations that sustain such a commitment are expressed in mutuality and welcoming. Hospitality involves an authentic partnership that resembles covenantal relationship. The covenantal dynamics are toward always greater inclusiveness, toward the stimulation of mutual giving and receiving. According to Luke Johnson, "We might call hospitality the catalyst for creating and sustaining partnerships in the Gospel. Within these partnerships all members, even God as director, will play the role of stranger."[15]

Paul's letter to Philemon abounds with the language of hospitality. Not only has Philemon made his home available, but he is known to be a specialist in hospitality. In this letter Paul is asking his friend, his partner, Philemon, to receive his runaway slave, Onesimus, as a guest and no longer as a slave, but as "a beloved brother...both in the flesh and in the Lord" (Phlm 16). This reception implies a transformed relationship, not only in relation to God but also in the socioeconomic world. Hospitality crosses the lines of the physical and the spiritual.[16]

Hospitality was a fundamental condition of the mission and expansion of the early church. The practice of hospitality is presented in the New Testament as the common virtue of the church. Like love, hospitality forges social bonds; it brings forth a sense of unity. There are many hints in the Pauline letters that ordinary Christians traveling to another city could expect to find accommodations with "brothers and sisters." The Christians are invited to accept strangers on trust and in faith. The church in the diaspora is to be as a home, *oikos,* for the *paroikoi,* the stranger. Such a practice is evident in the first letter of Peter.

By emphasizing the bipolar experience and symbols of isolation and community, homelessness and home, the letter challenges the Christian community to become a household in which fellowship can be established and sustained in an estranged world. Household constitutes a focus and locus for the Christian mission. The early Christians understood themselves to be members of "a family of faith" (Gal 6:10). All believers, former Gentiles and Jews alike, were "members of the household of God" *(oikeio to theou*) (Eph 2:19). All believing households together constituted the one "household of God" (1 Tim 3:15, cf. 3:4-5; Heb 3:6, cf. 10:21; 1 Pet 2:5; 4:17).

In 1 Peter the religious, theological, and spiritual meanings of the symbol "household of God" come to the fore and appear as a master Christian symbol. This is the case because of the existing need of many in Asia Minor. At the beginning of Christianity many saw themselves as alien and second-class citizens. They perceived themselves as existing in a hostile world. Peter's letter emphasizes the response to this experience of estrangement. "Above all, maintain constant love for one another, for love covers a multitude of sins. Be hospitable to one another without complaining. Like good stewards of the manifold grace of God, serve one another with whatever gift each of you has received" (1 Pet 4:8-10). Perceived as aliens, the early Christians lacked a sense of their communal identity and solidarity. "Beloved, I exhort you as resident aliens and visiting strangers to keep apart from the fleshly passions [of their Gentile background and environment] which wage war against you" (2:11, my translation). This negative warning is followed by positive encouragement: "Conduct yourselves honorably among the Gentiles, so that though they malign you as evildoers [as in 1:17], they may see your honorable deeds [again, as in 1:17] and glorify God when he comes to judge" (2:12).

In Peter the household (*oikos*) is used to address the issue of alienation. The *oikos* suggests familiar as well as familial imagery for depicting the social dimensions of life in the Kingdom of God. Household supplied "powerful social, psychological, and theological symbols for depicting the radical and comprehensive nature of Christian conversion and cohesion, the commonality of Christian values and goals, and the distinctive character of communal Christian identity."[17]

Here in this household those on the margins of society, the former outcasts, become the elect and privileged people of God. "But you are a chosen race, a royal priesthood, a holy nation, God's own people" (1 Pet 2:9). "The concept of the household served an integrative literary, theological, and sociological function."[18] Those without a home in society had the possibility of a home in the believing community; in the household of God all homeless have a home. The household of God functioned in 1 Peter as a potent symbol socially, psychologically, and religiously for articulating and integrating the expressions of faith and the experiences of life.

The formation of a new household of faith brings about a new order of values in which diverse peoples and classes are united. According to Ephesians 2:11-22, "the dividing wall, that is, the hostility between us" has been abolished. In this new household there are no longer strangers and resident aliens but fellow citizens. Christianity brings about a new vision of communal identity and solidarity.

What is affirmed in 1 Peter is of singular importance for Christians of every generation. Being a stranger in a hostile environment is for Christianity a divine vocation. Christians are resident aliens even as they are "called," "elected," and "sanctified." Christians, too, are strangers in the world, for God has given them a new home in heaven (Heb 11:15-16; Eph 2:6; Phil 3:20). In legal terms they belong to the city of God (Heb 11:10, 16; 12:22-23). They now have civil rights there (Eph 2:19). They are thus aliens in the world (John 15:19; 17:14, 16). They live as sheep among wolves (Matt 10:16). The world is offended by them (1 Pet 4:4). They can reside only as aliens in it (1 Pet 2:11). Christians belong to a new age, a new world. Their new home is beginning to take shape, yet it will be realized only in the future in a new age and new world. Hospitality is marked by eschatology. The Kingdom of God becomes a household for the strangers, where strangers, while still strangers, are no longer outcasts.

4. *"Kingdom of God" and Hospitality to the Stranger*

hristianity, the claim has been made, "is above all a way of seeing."[1] Seeing is all about images and imagination. Christian images and the Christian imagination are to be found in the scriptures; they imagine a world and provide images that nurture the Christian vision. Such images are rooted in the physical world and yet inhabit a deeper world. According to Luke Johnson, "People act on the basis of the imagined world in which they dwell, and by acting on what they imagine, they help establish their worlds as real."[2] What is being asked in this book is to imagine a world, a church, a human existence where hospitality to the stranger is the universal law and the universal practice. Again, according to Johnson, "To live within this imaginative world is not to flee reality but to constitute an alternative reality."[3] The scriptural imagination is prophetic; it offers to the world an alternative vision.

The central image of the vision of life sustaining the law of hospitality to the stranger for Christianity is that of the Kingdom of God. Jesus' central proclamation of the Kingdom constitutes a key element in New Testament understanding of hospitality. The fundamental image of the New Testament that creates, nourishes, and sustains the Christian vision is that of the Kingdom of God. That vision is articulated in the words of Mark's gospel, the first gospel, "The time is fulfilled, and the kingdom of God has come near; repent, and believe in the good news" (Mark 1:15). The fundamental reference of that image is the God of Jesus Christ.

There is a great irony in the choice of the words "Kingdom of God" by Jesus to express the object of our hope. As Walter Wink has indicated, the Hebrew root behind *king* and *kingdom* means "to possess, to own exclusively."[4] Wink describes the political system of kingship as "the domination system, a social system characterized by hierarchical power relations, economic inequality, oppressive politics, patriarchy, ranking, aristocracy, taxation, standing armies, and war. Violence became the preferred method for adjudicating disputes and getting and holding power."⁵ In Israel, kingship was always problematic. Having been oppressed by the domination system in Egypt, Israel desired to develop egalitarian politics and economics. The prophets resisted the kingship system adopted by Israel (1 Sam 8).

The Kingdom as the Activity of God

The central aspect of the teaching of Jesus was that concerning the Kingdom of God. This Kingdom is not a place or a thing but a deed. It is a verb not a noun—the activity of God. The Reign of God for Jesus means that God has chosen relatedness to persons as the only definition of the divine. God's being is being-with-us; in short, God is that unique "person" in the universe who makes a difference to all things and to whom all things make a difference. Jesus resisted the domination system. This is affirmed in Luke 22:24–27:

> A dispute also arose among them [the disciples] as to which one of them was to be regarded as the greatest. [Jesus] said to them, "The kings of the Gentiles lord it over them; and those in authority over them are called benefactors. But not so with you; rather the greatest among you must become like the youngest, and the leader like one who serves. For who is greater, the one who is at the table or the one who serves? Is it not the one at the table? But I am among you as one who serves."

In the Gospel of Mark, Jesus is presented as a servant, and discipleship demands a radical transformation of the domination system. The correlative of service is powerlessness. Power is to be measured within the community of disciples in terms of servanthood. Power is understood in terms of servanthood exemplified in Jesus' own servanthood. Such servanthood demands a letting go of possessions, of a possessive spirit.

In chapter 10 Mark tells us of the rich young man called to dispossess himself of material goods. This challenge closely resembles

Paul's affirmation, "For you know the generous act of our Lord Jesus Christ, that though he was rich, yet for your sakes he became poor, so that by his poverty you might become rich" (2 Cor 8:9). Possessions in this world are always an indication of power. As Luke Johnson writes: "Possessions do not merely express the inner condition of a man's heart; they are also capable of expressing relations between persons and the play of power between persons. Indeed, when all the aspects are brought together, power appears as reality which underpins them all. Possessions are a sign of power."[6] Jesus' beliefs about power are based on human experience, yet it is precisely because of this that the Kingdom is a mystery, radically overturning the expectations of this world. The Kingdom overthrows humanly constructed theology as well as human values with regard to the nature of power.

Jesus' remarkable rejection of domination is found in these words: "Blessed are those slaves whom the master finds alert when he comes; truly I tell you, he will fasten his belt and have them sit down to eat [literally, 'have them recline,' as at a formal banquet or feast], and he will come and serve them" (Luke 12:37). This is clearly not the way of the world. While in our midst, the Kingdom of God involves a transcendent dimension. It is God's work, and so it manifests, reveals God. Again while already present, it is also eschatological. While eschatological, the Kingdom of God is not simply otherworldly, for it brings about a social transformation. The image of the Kingdom of God has power to change and transform lives. As Paul wrote: "I am not ashamed of the gospel; it is the power of God for salvation to everyone who has faith" (Rom 1:16). Hope for salvation is summed up by Jesus in the expression "the Kingdom of God," or better, "the Reign of God." The Reign of God is the active lordship of God within ourselves and outside of ourselves.

What the Reign of God brings about is the reintegration of the poor and the marginal into society. The Kingdom of God contradicts any form of discrimination. As Sallie McFague writes, "The central symbol of the new vision of life, the Kingdom of God, is a community joined together in a festive meal where the bread that sustains life and the joy that sustains the spirit are shared with all."[7] The vision emphasizes radical inclusiveness: all are invited to the Kingdom of God.

The Christian vision expressed in the Kingdom of God is one of hope founded in compassion for the whole of humanity, especially for those who are at the margins of society. Jesus' announcement of the Kingdom of God is expressed in terms of welcome and warning. All are welcome, but especially the poor, the stranger, the marginal. Jesus offered a welcome to, and shared meals with sinners. The story of the Kingdom as told and enacted by Jesus invites its hearers to make it their own. The story of the Kingdom generates invitation, welcome, and challenge. The summons was shocking: Jesus' call overrode normal family obligations of the kind usually regarded as sacrosanct. The call offered nothing except a wandering life.

Jesus' summons to the Kingdom comes to a climax with the story of a rich young man (Luke 18:18–25). He came with a question: "What must I do to inherit eternal life?" Forsake riches and follow Jesus. Sell possessions. Jesus' summons is to risk all; his followers must "take up their cross and follow me" (Mark 8:34). Jesus' call challenges the existing familial and national symbolism: "Here are my mother and my brothers" (Matt 12:49). All those who respond favorably to Jesus' Kingdom announcement constitute a new family. The Kingdom of God, in principle open to all, beyond the border of Israel—land and family—is rethought in the promise that the eschatological blessing would reach beyond the traditional confines. This new family was of course characterized and marked out by one of the best-known features of Jesus' work: his open table fellowship with anyone who shared his agenda, who wanted to be allied with his Kingdom movement (Mark 2:13–17; Matt 9:9–13, 61).

The New Humanity

The author of Ephesians reminds us of the radical newness of Jesus' message:

So then, remember that at one time you Gentiles by birth, called "the uncircumcision" by those who are called "the circumcision"—

a physical circumcision made in the flesh by human hands—remember that you were at that time without Christ, being aliens from the commonwealth of Israel, and strangers to the covenants of promise, having no hope and without God in the world. But now in Christ Jesus you who once were far off have been brought near by the blood of Christ. For he is our peace; in his flesh he has made both groups into one and has broken down the dividing wall, that is, the hostility between us. He has abolished the law with its commandments and ordinances, that he might create in himself one new humanity in place of the two, thus making peace, and might reconcile both groups to God in one body through the cross, thus putting to death that hostility through it. So he came and proclaimed peace to you who were far off and peace to those who were near; for through him both of us have access in one Spirit to the Father. So then you are no longer stranger and aliens, but you are citizens with the saints and also members of the household of God, built upon the foundation of the apostles and prophets, with Christ Jesus himself as the cornerstone. In him the whole structure is joined together and grows into a holy temple in the Lord; in whom you also are built together spiritually into a dwelling place for God (Eph 2:11 -22).

The unity of Jew and Gentile in the one household is the starting point of a cosmic reconciliation: the summing up of all things in Christ. The coming of the Kingdom is the beginning of a new age in which Jew and Gentile, neighbor and stranger, are to be joined together without distinction in the people of God.

The author of Ephesians magnifies the understanding of the new humanity to a mystical height. Christ creates in himself one new home, one new household, his own body. Christ is the cornerstone, the mortar of this new household. He is the builder of this new home; the new humanity is a home-in-process. For Paul, the Kingdom of God is "righteousness and peace and joy in the Holy Spirit" (Rom 14:17). There is an unequivocal earthiness to this Kingdom, a reality with social dimensions in human history. Pauline faith and the faith of the whole New Testament consist in believing that the definitive Kingdom of justice and life has arrived. Jesus' ministry is concerned with the bringing about of this Kingdom of justice. According to Acts 10:38, Jesus "went about doing good and healing all who were oppressed by the devil." This healing ministry is simply the consequence of Jesus' compassion: "When...he saw a great crowd...he had compassion for them and he cured their sick" (Matt 14:14). According to Jon Sobrino, "The Reign of God is salvation because in its approach without ever arriving in fullness, it enables us to live as genuine human beings."[8] The Kingdom of God is addressed to all, but primarily to the poor. The Kingdom of God is a place that makes it possible for the poor, the outcasts, the strangers to have life and dignity. The Kingdom of God is a realm of hospitality.

In the New Testament hospitality centers upon meetings and transactions with strangers. This is also true of the Kingdom. The Kingdom is analogous to an open frontier. The Kingdom breaks in on meals, on the occasion of a parable understood and accepted, on the reception of strangers. It advances through alliance with strangers. In the eyes of Jesus the Kingdom often turns out to be both cause and consequence of *hospitality*. Encounters with strangers in the New Testament lead to partnerships, to co-participation in the power of the Kingdom, to companionship in building God's house and home. Hospitality to strangers has a generative power. The parables teach us about the character of Jesus' God, that God by nature recruits outsiders to be partners.

In the Kingdom of God strangers can be partners in spiritual blessings (Rom 15:27), in the gospel and grace (Phil 1:5-7), in mission (Gal 2:9-10), in service (2 Cor 8:23), in Christ's sufferings (Phil 3:10; 1 Pet 4:13), and in the suffering of others (2 Cor 1:7; Heb 10:33). Undergirding and empowering all of this is a fellowship with Christ (1 Cor 1:9; 1 John 1:3, 6), a communion of the Holy Spirit (2 Cor 13:14; Phil 2:1) into which believers are called by God (1 Cor 1:9).

Hospitality in the New Testament becomes the generative foundation for a particular way of existing. Fundamental to the building of partnership with strangers is a community that experiences itself as the guests of God. The controlling vision is that everyone must have a chance to share in the feast of the Kingdom and be welcomed into the new humanity. In the Kingdom, God's grace works among us to bring about a fair distribution of spiritual and material goods on all sides.

The Power of Powerlessness

The reversal demanded by the Kingdom of God has to do with a set of values expressed in the Beatitudes, in the attitude toward possessions, and in the commandment to love one's neighbor. Economic inequities are the basis of domination; power is intrinsically connected to wealth. "You cannot serve God and wealth" (Matt 6:24; Luke 16:13). In the Beatitudes, Jesus proclaims the ultimate power of poverty for the sake of the Kingdom.

The Sermon on the Mount (Matt 5:3–7:27; cf. Luke 6:17–49) is a synthesis of the implication and consequences of the Kingdom of God for the disciples' relationship with God, with others, and with the world. The Sermon on the Mount is a summary of the whole gospel. Its fundamental call is to be perfect as God is perfect, to love as the Father loves. "Be merciful, just as your Father is merciful" (Luke 6:36). In six antitheses Jesus indicates how the fulfillment of the Law can take place: "You have heard that it was said...but I say to you..." The fulfillment has to do with love: to forgive and to love even your enemy.

For Jesus, the *lex talionis,* "an eye for an eye and a tooth for a tooth," is no longer operative for the disciples; they are not to retaliate but to respond to evil with good. The spiral of violence cannot continue. In Matthew 5:39–42 Jesus gives five concrete examples about how radical one's forgiveness needs to be. All the examples imply an absolute and unconditional love of the "other." The imperative of love is limitless. According to verse 45, to love as God loves is to love without measure. Such love has much to do with our willingness to welcome the stranger as one of us. Such love is demanded because of the nature of God's love: God's love is limitless, unconditional, and all-merciful. In the Sermon of the Mount, Jesus is calling for an ethic of imitation. What is demanded of creatures is to become what God already is.

What are the implications of God's rule? And if, according to the message of the New Testament, the Kingdom of God is already in our midst, and has been inaugurated in and through Jesus' ministry, what difference does it make for society? The Sermon on the Mount is the expression of how the difference can happen: the ultimate power of powerlessness.

The radical aspect of Jesus' message is emphasized by the formula "blessed are you." All worldly blessings and values are to be considered of little worth in comparison to the blessings of the Kingdom of God. But the nature of the blessings involves a total reversal of values, expressed in relation to their recipients. The blessings are not for those who see themselves as virtuous but for the poor, the hungry, the sorrowful, the outcasts, and the powerless.

In his inaugural sermon in Nazareth Jesus can take up a saying of the prophet Isaiah (61:1) and proclaim that he has been sent to preach the good news to the poor, to announce the acceptable year of the Lord (Luke 4:18-19). The goodness of God passing all understanding means joy and gladness for the poor. They have received redress, before which all other values fade (Matt 13:44-46). They experience more than they have hoped for. God accepts them and, although they are empty-handed, Jesus himself rejoices with them.

Who are the poor to whom the Kingdom of God is promised? *Poor* is taken in a very broad sense; it includes the helpless, those without resources, those who suffer on account of their discipleship (Luke 6:22-23). Jesus' poor are those who have nothing to expect from the world but who expect everything from God. They are the ones who have been driven up against the limits of the world and its possibilities. They are beggars before God; only from God can they expect help.

In Favor of Neighbor

Jesus' proclamation of the Kingdom of God demands a radical decision in favor of our neighbor. His proclamation is related to the *shema,* with its dual command of God and neighbor: "Hear, O Israel: The LORD is our God, the LORD alone. You shall love the LORD your God with all your heart, and with all your soul, and with all your might" (Deut 6:4-6). For Jesus, the key phrase is "with all your soul," and it is encountered in the demand that we be prepared to sacrifice life itself: "If any want to become my followers, let them deny themselves and take up their cross and follow me" (Mark 8:34). Everything that Jesus said concerning our relationship to our neighbor is determined by the demand that we should be of help. Nothing may be allowed to stand in the way of care for our neighbor. Jesus' criticism of the scribes and Pharisees belongs to this context: "They tie up heavy burdens, hard to bear, and lay them on the shoulders of others; but they themselves are unwilling to lift a finger to move them" (Matt 23:4-5). Religious obligations have no priority here, not even the rules concerning the Sabbath. For Jesus, the Sabbath is for the sake of the people, and to serve God is to serve the people in their need.

Although everything in Jesus' proclamation centers around the Kingdom of God, God is not to be loved simply in liturgy and ritual but in care for our neighbor. The grace of God is compared to the gifts given by human beings. A man gets up in the middle of the night in order to give the help that has been requested (Luke 11:5-8). Jesus concludes: "How much more will your Father in heaven give good things to those who ask him!" (Matt 7:11).

The parable of the Good Samaritan (Luke 10:29-37) underlines the same point about the reality of the Kingdom of God, for it is given in the context of a question about eternal life. It leads away from questions about personal salvation to questions about the "other." Eternal life is in our midst as compassion.

In Luke, "neighbor" shifts from being the object of compassion (v. 34) to being the person who shows compassion (v. 36). But the Samaritan's compassion in no way springs from faith in Jesus. He does not act religiously. In Jesus' teaching, love of neighbor is not simply a means to the love of God, for this would not really be love. In the parable of the Good Samaritan, the help given to the one who has fallen among thieves is given strictly in response to his needs.

In this context the compelling question is, "Who is our neighbor?" In the story of the Good Samaritan, the scribe poses this question at a distance, as a theoretical problem, in the abstract. But such a question cannot be put in the abstract, because the neighbor cannot be put at a distance. The neighbor, then, is not simply a friend. It is anyone, friend or enemy. The love of Jesus invites his listener to break through all boundaries established by religion or nationality. God does not differentiate between friend and foe: "So that you may be children of your Father in heaven; for he makes his sun rise on the evil and on the good, and sends the rain on the righteous and on the unrighteous" (Matt 5:45-46).

The parable of the Good Samaritan teaches a radically new concept of neighborliness, one defined in terms of need rather than common membership in a racial or religious group. The Kingdom of God is in our midst. It manifests itself when compassion and forgiveness are offered to the one in need. Through the coming of the Kingdom of God everyone can now know that love is the ultimate; what is done out of love will endure forever.

The link between the Kingdom of God and the reception of this Kingdom in our lives is compassionate dedication to those in need. The *metanoia* demanded by the coming of the Kingdom of God takes concrete form in compassion. God's compassion and forgiveness precede and form the ground and source of our compassion to others. We are urged to be compassionate as God is compassionate; God's mercy is expressed here on earth in our mercy, just as God's compassion was demonstrated concretely in Jesus' compassion for the oppressed.

What of Possessions?

The resistance Jesus encounters to his message comes primarily from those who have possessions. In order to understand the meaning of possessions in the scriptures, it is important to grasp the physical and symbolic nature of human reality. According to Johnson, "The real mystery concerning possessions is how they relate to our sense of identity and worth as human beings. The real sin related to possessions has to do with the willful confusion of being and having."[9]

When it comes to possessions for a human being, the question of meaning is crucial; context is always essential. The important issue relative to possessions is what they mean to one who possesses.

Material possessions are not our being; they extend our beings into the world and into the lives of other persons. The scriptures remind us that they are truly gifts: "What do you have that you did not receive? And if you received it, why do you boast as if it were not a gift?" (1 Cor 4:7).

The Bible considers the use of material possessions significant for the life of faith. A cursory reading of the gospels shows the authors' concern about riches, poverty, and the use of possessions. "Take care! Be on your guard against all kinds of greed; for one's life does not consist in the abundance of possessions" (Luke 12:15). When Jesus called his disciples, as Luke tells us, "they left everything and followed him" (5:11). There is also the story of the young rich man who wanted to know the way to perfection. "Sell all that you own and distribute the money to the poor, and you will have treasure in heaven; then come, follow me" (Luke 18:22). The man withdrew sadly, for, as Luke notes, "he was very rich" (18:23). Jesus' comment on the whole situation was that it would be "easier for a camel to go through the eye of a needle than for someone who is rich to enter the kingdom of God" (18:24-25). "None of you can become my disciple if you do not give up all your possessions" (14:33). To become a disciple one is called to be radically poor, yet the disciples are also called to give alms. Along with the call to the radical renunciation of possessions, the gospels also invite to hospitality and to almsgiving. To provide hospitality to those in need, to the stranger, one must possess something.

Hospitality is creative of space, of home, for the guest. Within the Christian vision such a creative process is not without some ambiguity. Such creative hospitality demands some form of ownership. The question of hospitality and possession poses the fundamental question about how one uses possessions. In the scriptures individuals' responses to possessions are expressions of how they value reality, how they perceive and relate to the ultimate. In themselves, possessions are neither good nor evil. The issue is their use. The danger of ownership and of possession is challenged by the command of hospitality. While one must own in order to offer hospitality, hospitality protects from abusing ownership and possession. Hospitality to the stranger is a statement about how we perceive ownership and possession.

The basic attitude toward possessions required for authentic hospitality lies in the symbol of the crucifixion-resurrection. Crucifixion is the call to let go of all possessions, of life itself, the call to give up power and choose powerlessness in order for the other to receive life. Resurrection is the gift of life to the powerless (cf. Mark 5:1-20; Luke 19:1-10). The meaning of the cross/resurrection symbol is the proclamation of the end of the kingdom of domination and the coming of a new kingdom, a new home for the homeless. The new characteristics of the new kingdom are contrasted with the old, contrasts that include social, economic, and political concerns. This is stated in Mary's Magnificat.

> He has shown strength with his arm,
>> he has scattered the proud in the thoughts of their hearts.
> He has brought down the powerful from their thrones,
>> and lifted up the lowly;
> he has filled the hungry with good things,
>> and sent the rich away empty.
> He has helped his servant Israel,
>> in remembrance of his mercy,
> according to the promise he made to our ancestors,
>> to Abraham and to his descendants forever. (Luke 1:51-55)

The Greek word used for "the lowly" designates not only those who are without possessions, but those who are oppressed by their fellow human beings and must look to God for help. Luke points out the contrast between the rich man and the poor man (16:19-31). Their new situations are precisely inverted—the one who seems to possess all is now with nothing; the poor man is now the one comforted.

The Eucharist: Celebration of God's Hospitality

It is in the celebration of the Eucharist that the death and resurrection of Jesus are remembered and celebrated. It is in the Eucharist that one can find the primary resource for understanding

God, church, and world. The Eucharist within the church is the ritual occasion where Christians review and renew meanings and values. It is there that the radical implication of hospitality to the stranger can be understood and put into practice by every generation. According to Robert Bellah, the Eucharist "is the supreme ritual expression of brokenness and death, of homelessness and landlessness. It consecrates all the good things of the earth and it promises renewal and rebirth not only for the individual but for society and the cosmos. And yet it makes us restless on this earth: it makes us see the conditional, and provisional, and broken quality of all things human."[10] The ecclesial community, following the example given by Jesus, has as its central ritual a eucharistic meal.

The Spirit at work in the community does so in the form of agape, of love. Love is the great leveler. It is in the Eucharist that equality and reciprocity must be manifested. The conflict over the Lord's Supper in 1 Corinthians 11:20-22 is a conflict between rich and poor. "When you come together, it is not really to eat the Lord's supper. For when the time comes to eat, each of you goes ahead with your own supper, and one goes hungry and another becomes drunk. What! Do you not have homes to eat and drink in? Or do you show contempt for the church of God and humiliate those who have nothing?" At Corinth the chief sin, as Paul sees it, has to do with believers despising and humiliating one another. Receiving Christ's body and blood depends upon recognizing Christ "in the poorest." Those marginalized by social and economic injustice not only have a claim on God's mercy but an equally potent claim on the eucharistic community's attention.

Monika Hellwig captures the fundamental dimension of the Eucharist:

> The [Eucharist]...is in the first place the celebration of the hospitality of God shared by guests who commit themselves to become fellow hosts with God. It is the celebration of the divine hospitality as offered in the human presence of Jesus as word, wisdom and outreach of God. It subsumes in itself the grateful acknowledgment of God's hospitality in creation, but also the recall and renewal of God's liberating intervention on behalf of the *habiru* (Hebrews), the enslaved and deprived who had been kept from peoplehood,

freedom and human dignity, and were therefore redemptively called anew to be the People of God, a witness and blessing to all peoples of the earth.[11]

The celebration of the Eucharist is an affirmation of the community's solidarity with the poor, the aliens, and the marginalized people of the world. It is a pledge toward the full realization of the Kingdom of God; it is a sacrament of hope for the world, for the poor, and the coming about of the prophecy of the Magnificat. The sacramental integrity of the Eucharist is intrinsically connected to the preferential option for the poor. As Hellwig writes, "At the Last Supper Jesus makes it quite clear that to eat and drink of the unleavened bread and the cup of blessing is to enter into intimate fellowship with Him in his death—to accept what he does for them and to do this for others." The "new household of the Lord" is a covenantal community; it brings about a bond with Jesus Christ and draws it "in a new and intimate way into the great covenant of God with all mankind."[12]

The Eucharist is about food, about eating, but even more important, about sharing, for the food that the Eucharist is, is the "will of God," as Christ tells us. The will of God as revealed in Jesus Christ and as central to the Eucharist is to love God and to love our neighbor, even our neighbor-enemy, our neighbor-stranger. In fact, our love for our neighbor is a prerequisite of our love for God. This unity between love for God and love for humans is stated radically in 1 John 4:19–21:

> We love because he first loved us. Those who say, "I love God," and hate their brothers or sisters, are liars; for those who do not love a brother or sister whom they have seen, cannot love God whom they have not seen. The commandment we have from him is this: those who love God must love their brothers and sisters also.
>
> The commandment received in the Johannine community is, once more, the royal law, found on the lips of Jesus in John 15:12: "This is my commandment, that you love one another as I have loved you."

What is being affirmed, and in a mysterious way, is that only those who love their neighbor can know who God truly is. And only those who truly love God can share fully with the "other." Hospitality to the stranger is our way to God and God's way to us. Here God is not in competition with the neighbor-stranger but *is* the stranger. In the Eucharist the dialectic of host-guest is sacramentalized and realized; communion happens.

In the eucharistic celebration we recall Jesus' injunction to love one another as he has loved us so that the world may know that the Father has sent him. The Eucharist is a constant reminder of this mission. The mission is spelled out in the parable of the Good Samaritan spoken by Jesus in answer to the lawyer's question about who is his neighbor. The neighbor is anyone, and the neighbor in distress is God's call for compassion. The Samaritan "not only felt compassion ([Luke] 10:33) but expressed this compassion by his complete availability to the wounded man, where the man was; he literally had to step out of his own space into the place where the man lay hurting."[13] The Good Samaritan shared his possessions, shared himself; the way he responded to the wounded individual is the way he responded to God.

Strangers need not be enemies; in a sense we are all strangers like the Samaritan and the wounded individual. In an encounter with the stranger surprising things can happen. As Parker Palmer writes:

> The stranger of public life becomes the spiritual guide of our private life. Through the stranger our view of self, of world, of God is deepened and expanded. Through the stranger we are given a chance to find ourselves. And through the stranger, God finds us and offers us the gift of wholeness in the midst of our estranged lives.[14]

At the core of the eucharistic celebration is not only the expression of our hunger for love, but also the mystery of forgiveness and repentance. When the disciples of Emmaus invite the stranger into their home, they experience in the breaking of the bread a transformation. James Loder, referring to Luke 24:30–35, writes:

> As the two men "take this [broken bread] in," they are not only exposed to the brokenness they brought consciously to that room, but they are also exposed in the false hopes they brought into their

relationship with Jesus in the first place.... Thus the *broken body* received from the *risen* Lord presents a whole new reality, a startling way of looking at things.... Following Jesus' disappearance, the two men experienced a coalescence within and correlatively a power of new being.[15]

In the eucharistic celebration there is a moment for repentance, a moment during which the community needs to recognize the need for forgiveness. It is suggested that such a need for forgiveness has to do with hospitality. As a stance, hospitality, symbolized by the partaking of a meal, can set in motion a movement of awareness that leads to repentance.

Forgiveness is central to the paschal mystery, which is embodied in the Eucharist. Every Sunday the Eucharist is celebrated by thousands in the United States and yet America remains an unforgiving place. In a country where the death penalty has been a proven vote-getter in recent years, forgiveness is often seen as effete and irresponsible. Sometimes it even seems to condone the offense and the offender. And yet forgiveness is not for the weak.

The Eucharist is a time of special presence, a time in which diverse sorts of people can discover or rediscover their authentic humanity. Central to the Eucharist is the welcoming of the stranger, the building up of the new household of God. According to Victor Codina:

> The Eucharist is not simply a celebration of small historical victories, but a token of the final and full realization of the Kingdom of God. Thus it is not only a subversive memorial (J. B. Metz) [because it boldly proclaims that the present socioeconomic order is coming to an end] but a source of hope and the beginning of transfiguration. The bread and wine are transformed into bread and wine of the Kingdom, the beginning of the final utopia. And Jesus, eschatological mediator of the Kingdom, is made present with his transforming power. The epiclesis is not limited to the transformation of the gifts or of the community, but of all history into the body of the Lord.[16]

The eucharistic meal symbolizes so profoundly the building up of this household that Paul will not stand for any discrimination.

But when Cephas came to Antioch, I opposed him to his face, because he stood self-condemned; for until certain people came from James, he used to eat with Gentiles. But after they came, he drew back and kept himself separate for fear of the circumcision faction. And the other Jews [i.e., Jewish Christians] joined him in this hypocrisy, so that even Barnabas was led astray by their hypocrisy. But when I saw that they were not acting consistently with the truth of the gospel, I said to Cephas before them all, "If you, though a Jew, live like a Gentile and not like a Jew, how can you compel the Gentiles to live like Jews?" (Gal 2:11 -14).

Those marginalized by society have a strong claim on the eucharistic community's attention and hospitality. The truth of eucharistic participation depends on commitment to hospitality to the stranger, the means and the manner in which the Reign of God is actualized in our history.

5. The God of Hospitality

s a fundamental symbol expressing the Christian vision, Kingdom of God is all about God, not simply God alone but God-in-relation. Kingdom of God, communicated through parables, functions as a parable: it discloses something about God, about the world. Kingdom of God functions as a parable of reversal. As we have already seen, kingdom pointed originally to a domination system. Jesus in his parables and ministry offers his audience an alternative vision of kingdom. He portrays God as a compassionate God, welcoming, accepting, and forgiving. He offers a total reversal of the original meaning of kingdom and of the contemporary rule of Rome. The Kingdom of God is the opposite of all that Rome is; God's Kingdom belongs to the poor, the suffering, the persecuted, the powerless. These are the happy ones; the Kingdom belongs to them. In the Kingdom of God there is no longer a master-servant relationship: "I do not call you servants any longer, because the servant does not know what the master is doing; but I have called you friends" (John 15:15).

As we have already seen, Kingdom of God has much to say about possessions, poverty, and hospitality. The God of Jesus Christ must have much to do with those realities.[1] While God is neither Christian nor Hindu nor Muslim, there is a Christian way to God. That way is not simply a collection of doctrines but a person, the person of Jesus. The God of Christianity is the God of Jesus Christ, and the God of Jesus Christ is the God of Israel. God can be grasped and named in an abstract, metaphysical way; for example, the ungrounded ground of all reality, or, as Anselm formulated it, as "that which nothing greater can be thought." Rahner speaks of God as "Holy Mystery."[2] For Christians, this mystery revealed in the person of Jesus Christ is received, named, and celebrated as the paschal mystery. The paschal mystery emerges out of a series of particular historical events. As a complex of symbols, the paschal mystery is the expression of the experiences of a particular historical community. The paschal mystery as symbol seeks to bring to expression the manifestation of God in Jesus Christ.

Incarnation as Impoverishment

Christianity claims that in Jesus of Nazareth—in his life and ministry, in his death and resurrection—God is revealed. Central to this affirmation is the confession of John's prologue: "In the beginning was the Word, and the Word was with God, and the Word was God" (John 1:1-3). This confession has been expressed in the church as the incarnation. The belief that the Word of God, the eternal self-manifestation of the Creator, became flesh is fundamental to Christianity. Without the incarnation there is no Christianity. Incarnation means that the eternal Son of God, the eternal image, the icon of God has entered the world. Jesus is the human face of God. Karl Rahner writes:

> We Christians are the most sublime of materialists.... We recognize and believe that matter will last forever and be glorified forever.... [We believe that this world] is already filled with the forces of this indescribable transformation, this inner dynamism which Paul, speaking of the resurrection of the flesh, called the Holy Breath of God. We believe that this Spirit of God, this power of all powers, this meaning of all meanings, is now present at the very heart and center of all reality, including material reality, and has already, in the glorified flesh of Christ, brought the beginning of the world triumphantly to its...perfection. The universal and glorious transfiguration of the world...has already begun.[3]

The incarnation is the radical dispossession of God—a radical impoverishment "for our sake." When Paul appealed to the Corinthians to be concerned with the poor of Jerusalem, he motivated them with the following words: "For you know the generous act of our Lord Jesus Christ, that though he was rich, yet for your sake he became poor, so that by his poverty you might become rich" (2 Cor 8:9).

Commenting on this verse, Luke Johnson states:

It is likely that Paul is here referring to Jesus becoming human in
the first place, so that we are to read the "rich" as the preexistent
state of the Son, and the "poverty" as the incarnation. The taking
on of the human condition itself, then, was a form of impoverishment for the sake of others.[4]

This is also the case in Paul's letter to the Philippians.

> Let the same mind be in you that was in Christ Jesus,
>> who, though he was in the form of God,
>>> did not regard equality with God
>>> as something to be exploited,
>> but emptied himself,
>>> taking the form of a slave,
>>> being born in human likeness.
>> And being found in human form,
>>> he humbled himself
>>> and became obedient to the point of death —
>> even death on a cross. (Phil 2:5-8)

Christ did not "exploit" his status as God's Son as a possession,
but "emptied himself" by becoming human.

The incarnation is the self-emptying of Jesus that reached its com-
pletion on the cross. The cross was preceded by Jesus' ministry of
compassion and radical hospitality to the stranger. Jesus' ministry
was directed to replacing the domination system. The new alternative is the Kingdom of God, God's domination-free order. Jesus' origins, lifestyle, ministry, and attitudes in general do not sustain an
image of power and authority. His ministry is located among the
poor, the powerless, the social outcasts, the disreputable. He associates with lepers, sinners, and publicans. As revealed in the garden of
Gethsemane, where he accepts his cross, he has rejected any form of
power, human and ultimately even divine power.

Power, Service, Suffering, Compassion

Jesus' messianic program subverts the nature of power. The
Messiah becomes a servant; power is no longer domination but

service. This subversion is also evident in his use of the metaphor of the Kingdom of God to make evident God's gracious presence. In his parables and parabolic actions Jesus makes iconoclastic use of the metaphor of a kingdom, reversing it so that those at the bottom of the pyramid become the first in the Kingdom of God (Mark 10:14; Matt 19:30). The people without status are privileged members of the Kingdom of God. As Jon Sobrino has written:

> Jesus, in the specific historical reality of his life, conceived his mission in such a way that it had to follow a historical course leading inevitably to his being deprived of security, dignity, and life itself — the historical course of voluntary impoverishment. [The gospel shows us a Jesus who is gradually stripped of security, stripped of dignity, stripped even of his life.]
>
> What needs to be stressed in this objective process of impoverishment is that Jesus undertook it out of solidarity with the poor.... The five controversies in Mark 2:1–3:5 are based on a defense of the sick, sinners, and the hungry.... [Jesus'] impoverishment stems from something much deeper than asceticism. It stems from a voluntary solidarity with the poor and outcast.
>
> The requirements Jesus laid on others show that same movement in the direction of basic impoverishment: the call to follow him in order to carry out a mission in poverty, to leave home and family, to take up the cross.... This active process of impoverishment that Jesus practiced in his life is simply the historical version of what was later theologized as his transcendent impoverishment: the incarnation and kenosis [celebrated in the famous hymn in Philippians 2.6-11]. Note that this transcendent impoverishment took historical form not only through the assumption of human flesh, but also through the assumption of solidarity with the poor and outcast.[5]

Jesus' basic message about the Kingdom of God is a message about love. "Beloved, let us love one another because love is from God; everyone who loves is born of God and knows God. Whoever does not love does not know God, for God is love" (1 John 4:7-8). As we have seen such love is a hospitable love, love not only of the friend but *philoxenia,* love of the "other"—friend, stranger, even enemy. In such hospitable love one is born into the very life of God and having this life brings knowledge of God. It does this because God is love. Such love is unconditional.

In his ministry Jesus expresses a demand of absolute and unconditional love of others. Jesus invites us in our relationships to move away from self-centeredness and become centered on the "other." For Jesus, love is a chosen attitude that is translated into concrete gestures: to work for the good of all the persons who touch our life and also to pray for them, especially for those who have harmed us. The reason for such a radical stand is the very nature of Jesus' God and the nature of love. Such love allows no limits. Such love grounds the conviction of Paul that "neither death nor life, nor angels, nor rulers, nor things present, nor things to come, nor powers, nor height, nor depth, nor anything else in all creation, will be able to separate us from the love of God in Christ Jesus our Lord" (Rom 8:38–39).

In the Gospel of Matthew, Jesus describes how radical love needs to be: "You have heard that it was said 'You shall love your neighbor and hate your enemy.' But I say to you, Love your enemies and pray for those who persecute you" (Matt 5:43–45). In the Gospel of John, the two commandments are conflated into the single commandment of loving our neighbor. By loving our neighbor, even our enemy, we touch God's own reality, which is love.

The incarnation as an impoverishment is completed on the cross. The cross is the ultimate symbol of "becoming poor" for the "other." The *kenos* of Philippians 2 is about one who is enemy, who is handed over, who has given up possessions and has made himself poor. According to Paul, the preaching of the crucified Jesus is a folly for the world; it does not correspond to worldly experience. The death of Jesus was the death of a criminal; those who died crucified died outside the covenant. Jesus' death on the cross marginalized him. As John Meier writes:

> Any person declared a criminal by the highest authority of his or her society and accordingly put to death in a most shameful and brutal way at a public execution has obviously been pushed to the margins of that society. The ultimate impoverishment, the ultimate margin, is death, especially death by torture as a punishment meted out by the state for gross criminality. In Roman eyes, Jesus

died the ghastly death of slaves and rebels; in Jewish eyes, he fell under the stricture of Deut[eronomy] 21:23: "The one hanged [on a tree] is accursed by God." To both groups Jesus' trial and execution made him marginal in a terrifying and disgusting way. Jesus was a Jew living in a Jewish Palestine directly or indirectly controlled by Romans. In one sense, he belonged to both worlds; in the end, he was ejected from both.[6]

Jesus died an outcast because he had made himself an outcast. He ministered and ate with those who lived at the margins of society. As Walter Kasper writes, "The death of Jesus on the cross is not only the extreme consequence of his courageous ministry but a recapitulation and summary of his message. The death of Jesus on the cross is the final elucidation of what had been his sole concern: the coming of the eschatological reign of God."[7] Such an eschatological reality is described in Psalm 23:

> The LORD is my shepherd, I shall not want.
>> He makes me lie down in green pastures;
> he leads me beside still waters;
>> he restores my soul....
>
> You prepare a table before me
>> in the presence of my enemies;
> you anoint my head with oil;
>> my cup overflows.
> Surely goodness and mercy shall follow me
>> all the days of my life,
> and I shall dwell in the house of the LORD
>> my whole life long.

It is as the crucified one that Jesus is the symbol of God and the model for discipleship. The cross as symbol has the power to reveal God, to constitute community, and to energize Jesus' followers and change their beliefs and actions. "For Jews demand signs and Greeks desire wisdom, but we proclaim Christ crucified, a stumbling block to Jews and foolishness to Gentiles, but to those who are the called, Christ the power of God and the wisdom of God. For God's foolishness is wiser than human wisdom, and God's weakness is stronger than human strength" (1 Cor 1:22–25). God's action and presence are manifested at the point when Jesus is most clearly human. The weakness displayed on the cross is the power of God. Whatever we affirm about the divinity of Jesus cannot erase what was true of his authentic humanity. When we speak about incarnation, it must be recognized as an abasement and a mission. New Testament kenosis sees in Christ's full acceptance of the conditions of human existence the supreme manifestation of the limitless love of God for his unworthy creatures. When Paul wrote that "God proves his love for us in that while we were still sinners Christ died for us" (Rom 5:8), he summed up a truth inherent to the gospels.

Jesus' message about God was a message of good news about forgiveness and compassion. God does not stand outside the range of human suffering and sorrow. Jesus proclaimed a new presence of God. "In Christ God was reconciling the world to himself" (2 Cor 5:19). The christological hymn of Philippians 2:6–11 presents the self-emptying of Jesus as the revelation that to be God is to be unselfishness itself. In his life Jesus pursued a style of service even to the act of complete self-giving. Paul's discovery of the gospel was the discovery of the true character of divine power. In common with other Jewish disciples of Jesus, Paul would have expected God's Kingdom to be inaugurated by a "mighty act," but the death on the cross manifested not power but powerlessness (2 Cor 13:4). Its effect on Paul was one of radical conversion, a violent reversal analogous to that called for in Mark 10:42–45 and an abrupt realization that it is in Jesus' powerlessness on the cross that God's power is revealed.

God's power in the gospels cannot be understood except in terms of powerlessness, its apparent opposite. God's power is to renounce power. According to Mark, it is through God's power that Jesus is free to become powerless and submit to death. Dorothy Lee-Pollard describes this paradox:

> The divine power by which Jesus in the Gospel heals and liberates others is the same power by which he is able to renounce the power to save his own life.

So that breath-taking power to renounce power—to renounce what is most precious, what alone gives purpose and meaning to life, what lies at the core of one's identity—is precisely what reveals and actualizes the power of God. That is why the centurion recognizes who Jesus is in the blackness of despair of his own death.[8]

What is true of Jesus is also true of discipleship. God's power enables us to relinquish power. God can empower even the rich and powerful so that they are able to sacrifice wealth and power in the service of the poor.

Power, according to the paschal mystery, is not something to be retained or withheld; it is essentially relational and self-sacrificing. It is what Rollo May would call integrative power; it envisions mutuality and reciprocity. It is neither power over, power against, nor power for, but rather power with.

> The capacity to absorb and influence is as truly a mark of power as the strength involved in exercising an influence. Power is the capacity to sustain a relationship. This is the relationship of influencing and being influenced, of giving and receiving, of making claims and permitting and enabling others to make their claims.[9]

This model of power is relational where selves and groups emerge as realities. The magnitude of power consists in the range and depth of relationships that we can sustain. This includes relationships of receptivity, even of suffering; it is not the positing of will against will. Power is relation, and therefore the greater the power the greater the relation.

The goal of relational power is the creation and development of relationships. It does not intend, either directly or indirectly, to control the "other." It intends the enlargement of freedom; it is a commitment to the relational "us," to mutuality. Relational power, the capacity to sustain relationships, is not the business of management, control, or domination. Relational power is costly, however, for such power often involves suffering. In the Christian tradition the exact symbol of such a price paid is the cross, and the proper symbol of relational power is the Suffering Servant. Every true Christian reality passes through the crucible of kenotic love. Authority and power must necessarily do so.

Power that has been filtered through kenosis is never power from above but always power *with*. God's creative power never breaks in from the outside; it does not assent to the destructive facets of the human exercising of power. It is a power of love that challenges, releases, gives life. "Listen! I am standing at the door, knocking" (Rev 3:20); God does not force the door of our heart. Jesus' own *exousia* is characterized by precariousness and is experienced in the passivity of waiting; his power is the impotence of grace, the reconciling force of suffering, and the dominion of self-denying love.

God's works are accomplished in stillness and weakness, that is, in witness. The humility of the incarnation and the humble origins of every creature characterize God's work. They call for a certain affinity with God to notice and appreciate these things; weakness has an inner affinity with the living God, an affinity that power does not have.

God reveals Godself in the history of Israel and in Jesus' ministry as a compassionate God. In Israel, God is characterized as both a compassionate father and a compassionate mother. The intimacy and the loving attachment are related to the womb. Like the womb, divine compassion is life-giving; compassion creates the possibility for rebirth. God's compassionate love is a vital creative force. By compassion Jesus is brought to minister to the blind and the deaf. His miracles are signs of the inbreaking of God's compassionate reign. The disciples are called to compassion: "Be merciful, just as your Father is merciful" (Luke 6:36; Matt 5:48). Jesus offers the parable of the Good Samaritan to his disciples as an ideal upon which they should model themselves. The Samaritan "was moved to pity" at the sight of the wounded traveler (Luke 10:33). A more literal translation would be "moved in his spleen." Compassion is not only a question of understanding suffering but also of feeling the other's suffering in one's own life.

Compassion is not simply a feeling; it is primarily the capacity to enter into the joys and sorrows of another. The referent of compassion is always the "other." Compassion moves ministry beyond the confines of self-centeredness. Such symbols as the Exodus, Emmanuel, the incarnation, and the crucifixion allow ministry to be perceived as compassionate. Its power is compassionate power. Compassion is other-centered and self-sacrificing. It is grounded in a kenotic causality that exists both in nature and in the divine nature.

The partnership, the interdependence brought into being by God's presence in self-emptying, serves to reconcile the world through solidarity with the suffering and the oppressed. The one truly effective way to redeem people is the way of sociological incarnation, that is, by immersion in the wretchedness from which we need to be liberated. This solidarity by immersion becomes emancipatory, because it is ultimately humanizing. As disciples of the crucified and self-emptying Christ, we are drawn into his self-surrender, into his solidarity with the lost, his public suffering (cf. 1 Cor 1:26–31).

It is Jesus' vision that voluntary solidarity with the poor and the outcasts is precisely the means and the manner in which the reign of God is actualized. In the incarnation, God's hospitality is made flesh. Hospitality to the stranger and compassion for the poor become the way to the understanding of God's character (Luke 14:11; 12:37). Solidarity with the stranger is essential in the Kingdom of God. In the language of liberation theology, God as liberator acts in history to liberate all through opting for the poor and the oppressed of the present system. The poor, the downcast, those who hunger and thirst have a certain priority in God's work of redemption. Part of the signs of the Kingdom is that the lame walk, the blind see, the captives are fed, the poor have the gospel preached to them. Christ goes particularly to the outcasts, and they, in turn, have a special affinity for the gospel. But the aim of this partiality is to create a new whole, to elevate the valleys and make the high places low, so that all may come into a new place of God's reign, when God's will is done on earth. As Nathan Mitchell writes:

> Thus the very nature of God, for Jesus, is unconditional compassion towards the human world, unimpeachable love for creatures and creation. God is that One who cherishes people and makes them free. God's *will* is always and only a willing of good. God's *power* is always and only a power exercised on behalf of those who

need it—the poor, the outcast, the despised, the marginalized, the wretched and lonely, the abandoned.[10]

Poor is taken in a very broad sense; it includes the helpless, those without resources, those who suffer on account of their discipleship (Luke 6:22-23). Jesus' poor are those who have nothing to expect from the world, but who expect everything from God. They are the ones who have been driven up against the limits of the world and its possibilities. They are beggars before God; only from God can they expect help. The poor are the ones with whom Jesus associates—tax collectors, harlots, shepherds (Matt 21:32) or sinners (Mark 21:17), that is, the godless. The godless numbered people who ignored the commandments of God and were held up to contempt. The whole lot were lumped together as *am ha'aretz*—the poor, uneducated people who either did not know the complicated provisions of the Law or, if they did, could not keep them and were consequently despised by the pious. They were considered to be like Gentiles. While God's fatherhood extended to the Jewish people even when they were sinners, the same was not true for the Gentiles, who were sinners almost by definition. Gentiles lived apart from the Law. Jews who sinned could hope for mercy from their heavenly Father, but Gentiles could not count God as their Father.

Against this background we may appreciate the radical nature of Jesus' proclamation of the forgiveness of sins as expressed in the parable of the Prodigal Son. By becoming a swineherd, the son had made himself like a Gentile. Any Jewish father listening to Jesus' parable would have considered this son as dead. Yet in the parable the father forgives in an extravagant way. Here was a reversal, a situation in which God's love was being revealed in a new way. God is the compassionate one, and salvation is available to the most abandoned. The Kingdom of God cannot be contained by existing structures and institutions. God's holiness transcends clean and unclean, Jew and Gentile (or Jew who has made himself a Gentile). Jesus' table fellowship with sinners and the abandoned bears witness to the fact that Jesus, through his actions, carried his proclamation into effect.[11]

To understand what Jesus was doing in eating with sinners, it is important to realize that in the East, even today, to invite a person to a meal is an honor. It is an offer of peace, trust, brotherhood, and forgiveness; in short, sharing a table means sharing a life. In Judaism, in particular, table fellowship means fellowship before God; breaking bread shows that all who share the meal also have a share in the blessing the householder has spoken over the bread. Thus Jesus' meals with the publicans and sinners were not only events on a social level, an expression of his unusual humanity and social generosity, but they expressed his mission and message. The inclusion of sinners in the community of salvation, symbolized in table fellowship, is the most meaningful expression of the redeeming love of God.

What is revealed in Jesus Christ is that God has decided to journey with the totality of creation. Nothing and no one is excluded. In Christ, God is not to be seen as a self-enclosed, totally other reality. God can only be the hospitable God. As Jürgen Moltmann writes: "We are always inclined to perceive God, the Absolute, only in whatever is like ourselves. What is alien to us makes us uncertain. That is why we love what is like ourselves and are afraid of what is strange."[12] As the author of Hebrews advises, "Let mutual love continue. Do not neglect to show hospitality to strangers, for by doing that some have entertained angels without knowing it" (Heb 13:1-2). God is the stranger invited, excluded, turned away. God is no stranger to the stranger; God is a respecter of the other's otherness.

One cannot even pose a question about God without the existence of a community for which such a question is of concern. It is the existence of such a community that is in question today. In whatever form the Christian community takes, it stands in relationship to the event that authorizes it: Jesus Christ. Christianity cannot be a matter of the transmission of an unchanging "content" of faith. It must be a matter of a certain practice of transmission itself, a practice routed in Jesus' practice whereby one must constantly receive from a past and give to a future in a manner that makes way for that which is "different," a style of existence that "permits" a move of creativity and opens a new series of experiences.

To exist as a Christian is not simply to live as a lonely soul facing Jesus; rather, it is an existence lived out in the midst of the concrete others who make up the human community. One cannot be a Christian without the event of Jesus, to whom one is related through faith, or without the others of the community, to whom one is related through love. In the unity of faith and love Christians live in the absence of the historical Jesus, but in the presence of others. For it is in the communal structure of the Christian faith, in its irreducible plurality of witnesses, in its conflict and solidarity that one encounters the divine Other.

As we have seen, the Gospel of Luke imposes on the disciples, on those who have possessions and power, an indispensable requirement quite at odds with the social values of their own society and even more so of our own society. God "has brought down the powerful from their thrones, and lifted up the lowly; he has filled the hungry with good things, and sent the rich away empty" (Luke 1:52-53). Chapter 14 recalls that magnificent guests are to sit in the lowest place "for all who exalt themselves will be humbled, and those who humble themselves will be exalted" (v. 11). A host is to invite not the rich but the poor who cannot reply (vv. 13-14). In the parable of the Great Banquet, opening with a phrase from the Lord's Prayer about eating bread in the Kingdom of God (v. 15), the poor are invited.

In sending the Twelve on a mission, Jesus admonishes: "Take nothing for your journey, no staff, nor bag, nor bread, nor money—not even an extra tunic. Whatever house you enter, stay there, and leave from there. Wherever they do not welcome you, as you are leaving that town shake the dust off your feet as a testimony against them" (Luke 9:3-5). The disciples are to rely solely upon the material hospitality offered by those who accept their ministry. The first believers had all in common and were of one mind and heart because of the presence of the Holy Spirit: "There was not a needy person among them" (Acts 4:34). Luke is presenting an idealized and utopian view against which later communities could measure themselves.

Emphasis on hospitality in the founding church led to a community where all was shared in common. Originally the entire

Christian community needed to be hospitable (Rom 12:13). In 3 John 5:8 hospitality is presented not as a work of charity but also as a participation in the ministry of the word. As the church moved away from its original fervor and hospitality became less prevalent in Christian households, bishops, who originally had hospitality as a particular task (cf. 1 Tim 3:2), invited specific groups, especially monks, to establish hospices for programs for the poor and the sick. These institutions were named *xenodochion,* and hospitality became a characteristic of monastic institutions. In St. Benedict's Rule, for example, two chapters are dedicated to hospitality, which is perceived as a form of ministry.

The Christian vision as expressed in the Kingdom of God demands the emergence of a new community, a new place. In Ephesians 2 Paul urges the early Christians to create a space where "you are no longer strangers and aliens, but you are citizens with the saints and also members of the household of God, built upon the foundations of the apostles and prophets, with Christ Jesus himself as the cornerstone" (Eph 2:19-21).

The ecclesial community needs to be a home for the homeless, a house for the stranger, the house of the spirit, *oikos pneumatikos.* The new community is to be "my Father's house" (John 14:2).

> You are my friend if you do what I command you. I do not call you servants [slaves] any longer, because the servant does not know what the master is doing; but I have called you friends, because I have made known to you everything that I have heard from my Father (John 15:14-15).

Membership in the household of God entails an intimate degree of familial relationship. Those who are of the "house of God" are the "children of God," brothers and sisters of the Lord and in the Lord. Admission to this household is described as an act of adoption.

> But when the fullness of time had come, God sent his Son, born of a woman, born under the law, in order to redeem those who were under the law, so that we might receive adoption as children. And because you are children, God has sent the Spirit of his Son into our hearts, crying, "Abba! Father!" So you are no longer a slave but

a child, and if a child then also an heir, through God (Gal 4:4-7; cf. Rom 8:14-17).

The household that really matters for Christianity is the household of faith; a gathered community from the nations of the world. "Who are my mother and my brothers?... Whoever does the will of God is my brother and sister and mother" (Mark 3:33).

Paul refers to Christ's church as "the family of faith" (Gal 6:10) and the "building" or temple of God (1 Cor 3:9-17; 6:19-20). What Christians accomplish in sharing with one another is the "building up of a dwelling" (*oikodomein*), the house of both a fellowship and a place of meeting (cf. 1 Cor 1:16; Acts 11:14; 16:15). The spirit builds up the community house; *oikodomein* is a community concept that is understood teleologically, spiritually, cultically, and ethically. Fundamental to the new humanity in Christ is a fluid tension between unity and equality among believers. Paul's emphasis is on unity; the process is the incorporation of diverse peoples into the one body of Christ. This does not imply that all divisions will disappear (cf. Gal 2:11-14).

The passing away of slavery, racism, and sexism is clearly meant to be an eschatological truth. Yet incorporation in the one body of Christ intends transformation, change not only spiritual but also socioeconomic. "For Paul, the gospel requires that we see God and therefore ourselves as God's dwelling place, actively at work in reversing the conventional hierarchy of this age."[13]

> Consider your own call, brothers and sisters: not many of you were wise by human standards, not many were powerful, not many were of noble birth. But God chose what is foolish in the world to shame the wise, God chose what is weak in the world to shame the strong; God chose what is low and despised, and things that are not, to reduce to nothing things that are, so that no one might boast in the presence of God. (1 Cor 1:26-29)

Hospitality is how this house of God functions. Christianity, according to 1 Peter, was offering a unique kind of hospitality: equality to all within a society obsessed with the love of prestige. Acquisition of equality and status becomes all the more attractive to the stranger in particular. In the situation of social estrangement the stranger is forced to come to grips with his or her strangeness. The predicament of estrangement involves, among other things, diminished access to the generally recognized means for acquiring security, social acceptance, and prestige. The Christian community is to be characterized by its communal dimension and complete restructuring of all personal relationships, by the absolute value given to compassion, by its transformative nature and redemptive solidarity; inclusively as such the ecclesial community founded in Christ is truly the house of Spirit, for the Spirit is at work in this house.

The Spirit's function is to gather together that which is separated: creation, humanity in general, individual men and women. This gathering is achieved through incorporation into that which is deepest in God. The Spirit, the bond of love between the Godhead and Christ, also binds every relationship between God and humanity. The Spirit is the bond between persons, the source of social as well as divine unity. The Spirit is the source of all *koinonia,* of all communion. The Spirit is the creator of the particular *koinonia* we name church. The church is the sacrament not only of Jesus Christ but also of the Spirit. Through the kenosis of the Holy Spirit the church is established. By the kenosis of the Spirit the church is given gifts, charisma, and creativity. Pentecost makes manifest the activity of the Holy Spirit: creating communion in diversity, institution, and charisma. Continuity and creativity compose the church and its dynamic. In community the Spirit makes room for Christian freedom, for unity in difference. The Spirit makes inconsequential our differences of race, religion, social status, and gender.

Communion in love is not uniformity but union in difference both among human beings in general and between each particular person and God. Union in the Spirit preserves and perfects humanity precisely in its finite individuality and otherness. The positive aspect of the finite world precisely in its radical "otherness" before the infinite God is grounded in the inner trinitarian otherness that unites the Godhead with Christ in the Spirit. The community created by the Holy Spirit is respectful of the manifold differences in human existence. Unique aspects of individual personality that contribute to a person's growth are welcomed and nourished in a Spirit-filled community. The infinite worth of the finite human creature is thus established and preserved. It is not destroyed horizontally either by the sacrifice of the individual for the common good or by the transferral of significance from the individual to the family, the nation, or humanity in general. It is not destroyed vertically by the dissolution of the finite human spirit into the infinity of the Godhead or by the self-absolutizing of the finite into the infinite. Communion and respect for otherness are the authentic marks of a Spirit-filled community, where each person makes room in love for the freedom proper to others. To enter into genuine union is to respect the other's true freedom and uniqueness. It is the "go-between," God the Holy Spirit, that makes possible this shared existence, this dynamic emancipatory coherence. The church is called to make manifest the community and unity of the Trinity. The Trinity is a community where there is neither superiority nor subordination. The kenotic church is characterized by the same *perichoresis,* the dynamic process of making room for another around oneself. Perichoresis emphasizes relatedness and communion.

The vision of the church at Vatican II was that of communion. Indeed, the Roman Synod of 1995 affirmed that this vision was the council's most important teaching. Both communion and community derive from the Greek *koinonia. Koinonia,* in turn, comes from *koinos,* "common," and the verb *koinoun* means "to put together." *Koinonia* and its Latin cognates *communion* and *communicatio* indicate the action of having in common, of sharing in and participating in. Robert Kress reminds us that the real sense of these words is one of participation, solidarity, and responsibility. *Communion,* unlike *community,* is an active word. It involves active and mutual communication. Moltmann's understanding is that "we give one another life and come alive from one another. In mutual participation in life, individuals become free beyond the boundaries of their individuality."[14] Yet without kenosis we cannot have communion, nor can we experience the unity that respects diversity. Communion as perichoresis is achieved through self-emptying yet going out to the "other," fully respecting the otherness of the "other."

The community engendered by the Spirit can be neither exclusive nor hermetic. The Lucan account of Pentecost supposes an intentional universality of the gift of the Spirit. The message entrusted to the apostles is destined for all, given to all as the point where the divine enters and is received. No person or community has a monopoly on the Holy Spirit: "The wind [Spirit] blows where it chooses, and you hear the sound of it, but you do not know where it comes from or where it goes" (John 3:8). No person or institution can possess the Spirit, for it blows where it pleases. The bestowal of the Spirit—whether upon Jesus or upon a community—is always for a universal purpose; it is for the benefit of all. In fulfilling its nature the church must reenact the compassion of the prophets. Its compassion must be universal. It shall not discriminate between those who are members of the church and those who are not; it shall not choose between friends and enemies. Its compassion must be unconditional and inclusive. It must not be ethnocentric, denominational, nationalistic, or chauvinistic in any way.

Pilgrimage is the metaphor that best describes the ecclesial community in a world where so many are physically and spiritually homeless. Not only is this community "on the road," but it is also a place of pilgrimage. "Places of pilgrimage are as a rule more hospitable to the strange and the stranger than institutions entrenched in one particular community."[15] In a place of pilgrimage, pilgrims of all races and social strata leave behind their particular cultural milieux; they become a new community on the way.

According to Luke Johnson:

The image of a people on pilgrimage is obviously more persuasive when congregations move in liturgical procession through streets and fields on rogation days, chanting the litany of all those saints who form "the cloud of witnesses" waiting at the end of their journey toward God, or when they follow the "light of Christ" that is the Paschal Candle through the darkened nave at the Easter Vigil, or when they visit the sick and elderly to bring the eucharistic bread as *viaticum,* or when they pray in the manner of the *Cloud of Unknowing* or the *Way of the Pilgrim,* or when they walk through the streets seeking the homeless and providing them with shelter in their church building. Such practices of piety make the metaphor of "being on the way" an interpretation of lived human experience, and bring the world imagined by Scripture into existence by embodying it in the physical space we humans share with each other.[16]

The community engendered by the Kingdom of God is a home in process. Regard for strangers in their vulnerability and delight in their novel offerings presuppose that we perceive them as equals, as people who share our common humanity in its myriad variations. Since the basis of their true home is no longer kingship or a common history and culture but grace, we are less in need of familiar places and customs to stabilize our individual and corporate identities. We can become a pilgrim people, finding new companions in our life-journey from every race and nation and from every social stratum. We are summoned to community in which no particular manner of dwelling enjoys special privilege. The only requisites are that freedom be maintained and community fostered and plurality celebrated.

In its metaphorical usage, hospitality does not refer simply to literal instances of interaction with people from societies and cultures other than our own. It suggests attention to "otherness" in its many expressions: wonder and awe in the presence of the holy, receptivity to unconscious impulses arising from our being, openness to the unfamiliar and unexpected in our most intimate relationships. Identity and plurality, unity and diversity, the familiar and the strange, seeing through one's own eyes and seeing through the eyes of another, being at home in the world and being a pilgrim in a strange land negotiating a common world and honoring plurality—these are the motifs that characterize our new space, the household of the Lord.

CONCLUSION

A basic issue confronting our contemporary world is the conception of the self. Is the modern self fragile and fragmented? The Christian vision demands a very specific kind of self. The welcoming of the stranger is not a pious, easy act of generosity that will be uniformly approved. To welcome the stranger today is to challenge the social arrangements that exclude and include; it is to challenge the conception of the self as primarily individual.

If anything is evident in Christianity's valuing of hospitality to the stranger, it is that love is the core value of Christian life. This love is characterized by compassion. It is also unlimited love; that is, a love with no strings attached. When it comes to compassionate love, there can be no question of passive, silent spectatorship. There is nothing soft or naive about compassionate love lived in a harsh and unjust world. The Christian vision demands the formation of a specific kind of self, a hospitable self. The hospitable self is marked by the paradox of the Christian vision: "Those who find their life will lose it, and those who lose their life for my sake will find it" (Matt 10:39). Compassionate love is not always met with love; often it is rejected and even crucified. The hospitable self is a suffering self; this self calls into question many of our impulses toward selfishness, rivalry, and aggression. The hospitable self is a compassionate self. To be compassionate is not simply an ethical commitment; it is a behavioral and attitudinal stance. It reflects the deep metaphysical awareness that we are all brothers and sisters in a sense that is infinitely richer than the merely biological. When I touch another in authentic compassion, I break through the veil of illusion produced by the selfish self.

The primordial experience of the hospitable self is that of creatureliness. As a creature the self must inevitably center itself in this world. The basic issue is the mode of centering. This centering

activity cannot be simply an expression of power, of taking possession. We stand before God as creatures; in a real sense we *possess*
nothing.

Scripture affirms humanity as created in God's image and
Christ as the perfect image of God. In accepting the affirmation
that we are created in the image of God, it is our creatureliness
that needs to be emphasized. Creatureliness underlies the fact
that our very humanness emerges as a reality that is contextual,
embodied, and conditioned. The claim of the "other" is essential.
Creatureliness, by essence, implies the notion of gift and grace.
There is always, at the root of all that is, a receiving and a giving.
These can never be eliminated. There is an original social nature
of being from which and by which each person becomes more a
person. Singularity and particularity are consequences of historical and social existence. Even in relation to God, Adam cannot be
complete without encountering himself in the "other." This relational dimension of existence underlies the graciousness as well
as the precariousness of the process of becoming human.

The "I" cannot exist without the "you," and it cannot develop its
inherent singularity without a significant "Thou." The dignity and
integrity of personal humanness are determined by the "other." The
self is constituted as a person in its encounter with another. This
encounter, which constitutes the individual's own personhood,
implies an unconditional invitation to acknowledge the other,
encountered as a person with his or her own dignity and integrity.

The refusal of creaturehood involves the refusal to be interdependent, the avoidance of the limiting conditions of relationship;
it denies the possibility of being shaped by something other than
our own choice; it is the refusal of indebtedness. Creatureliness,
and therefore contingency, historicity, and finitude characterize
human existence. An anthropology built on the concept of creation in the image of God must be marked by the same characteristics. Human beings are understood to be created in the image of
God and re-created in the image of God in Jesus Christ. This
"given" possesses a nature, which is submitted to history and contingency and which has need of development and process. It is the

person in society and in nature, in mutual reciprocity, who is the image of God.

Personal life emerges in the encounter of person with person or personal otherness with personal otherness. Emphasis on creatureliness stresses the pervasiveness of relationality in the structure of everything. The individual is constituted by relationships at all levels. To accept the status of creature is to accept limits as opportunities. To accept the necessity of receiving from others, of relating without acquisitiveness or manipulation, is a kenotic understanding of humanness.

Creation, therefore, is the decentering of the self. Its focus is the "other," the neighbor in whose advent we know ourselves. We cannot responsibly avoid relationship. The advent of the other reveals that our freedom, insofar as it relates only to itself, is arbitrarily created and is determined by both the physical and the social.

The basic fact of our human condition is that we are servants of one another, which implies that each of us values all others for themselves. No one outgrows dependence on others or being-for-others. Relational thinking does not posit an ontological difference between realities, including God. It assumes an ontological sameness insofar as the primary kenotic principle of becoming has its verification in all that actually is. In a relational world metaphysical sameness contains the possibility of an infinite degree of variation. From a relational perspective all that actually is is interdependent.

Love is at the source of personhood. To exist as a person is to be referred to others. Total self-reference brings about the negation of love; dissolution of personhood implies the inability to love. Love is the existential component of personhood. The capacity to love is the capacity to place another within the reality of self-existence in such a way that real modification occurs for each. One can indeed say that the essence of the person is love. True personhood is an entering into community with the other or a surrendering to the other. One becomes a person by loving oneself in the other. In the process of self-emptying the self is enriched and embodied in its presence to others. The person is the bringing together of universality and particularity, the possibility of at once eliminating and possessing distinction.

In the Christian way the crucial decision regarding God is made in our relationship to one another. The place for trusting surrender to God is in the love of our neighbor. When we love kenotically, the other is radicalized. The New Testament affirms that one who loves one's neighbor has fulfilled the Law. This is the ultimate truth: God has been one's neighbor. In the kenotic life everyone is our neighbor, whoever happens to be at hand, unconditionally, without discrimination. This is why a kenotic love involves the enemy.

Christian love is love of the unworthy, the worthless, the lost. The love of neighbor does not arise from nor is it proportional to anything we possess or acquire. Such a love is based neither on favoritism nor instinctive aversion. There can be no exclusiveness, no partiality, no elitism. Kenotic love is characterized, essentially, by its universality; it is the foundation of interdependence. Interdependence is a way of being, of existing without mastery, without force, without difference in status. In interdependence whatever is superior demonstrates its superiority by its power to empty itself. The abundance of interdependence in reality is revealed in the humiliation of the exalted and the exaltation of the lowly.

The interdependent life is one of radical mutuality and reciprocity, of receiving and of giving, so completely for and from the other that nothing is left of self-centeredness. The deepest center of the self is always beyond the individual ego. Human suffering at its deepest level is not the self-suffering of isolated monads.

"For-otherness" constitutes the person as person. A self turned toward others finds its fulfillment. The issue of authentic selfhood turns on the issue of love for neighbor. We are authentic selves only in direct proportion to our ability to be affected by and related to others. The substance-self of the classical tradition is at best an abstraction. I am the person I am precisely because of my relationship to this history, this family, these friends. I am a profoundly relative, not substantial, being. Whether I know it or not, I am the person I am because this friend, person, idea has entered my life.

77

While for-otherness is constitutive of personhood, so is from-otherness. That we derive from others, that we live from others, is fundamental. It is through being loved that we learn to love; we have to receive in order to be able to give. A breakdown in this basic from-otherness may lead to a radical breakdown of self. Since we are neither autonomous nor self-sufficient, we have to receive simply in order to be. Interdependence is the basic structure and dynamic of personal existence. The interdependent life is made up of mutuality, exchange, and reciprocity.

There is no love without compassion. One who is compassionate manifests human solidarity by crying out with those who suffer, by feeling deeply the wound of the other. Compassion invokes our consciousness of the unity of the human race, the knowledge that all people, wherever they dwell in time and space, are bound together by the human condition. Nothing human is foreign to us. This sense of self is not based on an understanding of how and where we differ, but on how we are the same. Personal identity is found in the common experience of being human, in compassion, in suffering with others, in real love. Compassion does not lead to commiseration but to comfort, to being strong with the other.

"Hospitality to the stranger" is a shortcut formula expressing the core of the Christian vision. While it implies certain doctrines, it is primarily a practice, a way. It is the way of Jesus. It is the way of and to the Kingdom of God. While the Kingdom of God is gracious, God's own doing, the Kingdom entails and demands a practice. In fact, without the practice Jesus demanded and realized, the Reign of God cannot be understood. The Kingdom of God is not for spectators. In giving hospitality to the stranger appears all the alienation and injustice of homelessness. In sharing with the dispossessed appears the cruelty of oppression. It is in practice that the destructive nature of the anti-Reign appears. The anti-Reign is still in our midst: the millions of refugees and the increasing difficulties of immigrants coming to our shores and the oppressing nature of immigration laws demonstrate this. The presence of the anti-Reign is evident in the growing anti-immigrant feeling that has emerged worldwide. The practice of hospitality to the stranger as advocated in Matthew 25 is not only an obvious ethical demand but also a hermeneutical principle of comprehension. Practice reveals the Reign of God; it is anchored in an implicit yet comprehensive vision of reality. Such a vision "encourages a diaspora ethics of itineracy, detachment, dispossession, solidarity, and endurance in suffering, rather than a homeland ethics of stability, engagement, acquisition, and human fulfillment in the present life."[1] Such a vision calls into question our impulses toward selfishness, rivalry, and aggression. It challenges our constricted vision; it represents an assault on the accepted conventions, including the social, economic, and mythic structure that we build for our own comfort and security. Matthew 25:31-46 inverts and subverts accepted ways of being and suggests that the way of the Kingdom is not the way of the world. In Jesus' teachings we hear about a feast that is given for the poor and the outcasts, about a stranger who comes to the aid of an enemy. We hear that attempts at separating the worthy from the unworthy, dualisms such as rich/poor, Jew/Gentile, elder/younger—and by implication, male/female, white/nonwhite, Christian/non-Christian—are without basis in the vision of existence alluded to by the phrase *Kingdom of God*. While such a vision attracts and repels by its radicalism, it is the way Jesus chose. It is the "road less traveled" and yet the necessary road; it is not an unattainable way, yet one to be realized progressively. In the Kingdom of God we are all adolescents, on the way.

NOTES

INTRODUCTION

1. Edward Farley, *Deep Symbols: Their Postmodern Effacement and Reclamation* (Valley Forge, Pa.: Trinity Press International, 1996), 57.

CHAPTER ONE
HOSPITALITY TO THE STRANGER: PUTTING IT IN PERSPECTIVE

1. Homer, *The Odyssey*, trans. Robert Fitzgerald (Garden City, N.Y.: Doubleday, 1961), 233.

2. Ibid.

3. Mary Douglas, "The Idea of a Home: A Kind of Space," in *Home*, ed. Arlene Mack (New York: New York University Press, 1993), 271.

4. Alfred Schulz, "The Homecomer," in *Collected Papers*, vol. 2, *Studies in Social Theory*, ed. A. Brodersen, Phaenomenologica 15 (The Hague: Martinus Nijhoff, 1964).

5. Jürgen Moltmann, "The Home of the Homeless God," in *The Longing for Home*, ed. Leroy S. Rouner (Notre Dame, Ind.: University of Notre Dame Press, 1996), 172.

6. Walter Brueggemann, *The Land: Place as Gift, Promise and Challenge in Biblical Faith* (Philadelphia: Fortress Press, 1977), 107.

7. Gaston Bachelard, *The Poetics of Space*, trans. Maria Tolas (Boston: Beacon Press, 1969), 112.

8. Katherine Platt, "Places of Experience and the Experience of Place," in Rouner, *The Longing for Home*, 113.

9. James Duncan, "The House as a Symbol of Social Structure," in *Home Environments*, ed. Carol Werner (New York: Plenum Press, 1985), 148.

10. Rosemary L. Haughton, "Hospitality: Home as the Integration of Privacy and Community," in Rouner, *The Longing for Home*, 212.

11. Ibid.

12. Ibid., 215.

13. Henri Nouwen, *Reaching Out* (Garden City, N.Y.: Doubleday, 1975), 51.

14. Parker J. Palmer, *The Company of Strangers: Christianity and Renewal of America's Public Life* (New York: Crossroad, 1981), 68.

15. Ibid., 69.

16. Haughton, "Hospitality," 17.

CHAPTER TWO

HOSPITALITY TO THE STRANGER IN AMERICA

1. David Hollenbach, "The Common Good and Urban Poverty" in *America* 180/20 (June 5-12, 1999), 8-11.

2. Palmer, *The Company of Strangers*, 21.

3. Hollenbach, "The Common Good and Urban Poverty," 9.

4. Stephen L. Carter, *Civility, Manners, Morals, and the Etiquette of Democracy* (New York: Harper Perennial, 1998), 102.

5. Ibid.

6. Robert Bellah, *The Broken Covenant* (New York: Seabury Press, 1973).

7. Mark Searle, "The Notre Dame Study of Catholic Parish Life," in *Worship* 60 (July 1986), 333.

8. Christopher Lasch, *The Culture of Narcissism* (New York: W. W. Norton Co., 1978), 34.

9. Ibid., 232.

10. Ibid.

11. See Ernest Becker, *The Denial of Death* (New York: The Free Press, 1973).

12. Richard Dawkins, *The Selfish Gene* (New York: Oxford University Press, 1976), 2.

13. Ibid., 3.

14. C. R. Hogan, "Theoretical Egocentricism and the Problem of Compliance," *American Psychologist* 5 (1975), 533-40.

15. Ibid.

16. Phillip Rieff, *The Triumph of the Therapeutic: The Uses of Faith After Freud* (New York: Harper & Row, 1966).

17. Erich Fromm, *Man for Himself: An Inquiry into the Psychology of Ethics* (New York: Rinehart & Co., 1947), 7.

18. Cf. Carter, *Civility, Manners, Morals, and the Etiquette of Democracy*.

19. Brueggemann, *The Land*, 1.

CHAPTER THREE
THE FOUNDATIONS OF HOSPITALITY TO THE STRANGER

1. Brueggemann, *The Land,* 59.
2. Ibid., 189.
3. Ibid.
4. Ibid.
5. Luke T. Johnson, *Sharing Possessions* (Philadelphia: Fortress Press, 1981), 94.
6. Brueggemann, *The Land*, 14.
7. Ibid., 47.
8. Ibid., 57.
9. Ibid.
10. Ibid.
11. Hans Frei, *The Identity of Jesus Christ* (Philadelphia Fortress, 1975), 29–30.
12. John Koenig, *New Testament Hospitality* (Philadelphia: Fortress Press, 1985), 9.
13. Joachim Jeremias, *The Eucharistic Words of Jesus* (New York: Charles Scribner's Sons, 1966), 205.
14. Thomas Merton, *The Collected Poems of Thomas Merton* (New York: New Direction Books, 1977), 383.
15. Johnson, *Sharing Possessions*, 10.
16. John H. Eliot, *Home for the Homeless* (Philadelphia: Fortress Press, 1981), 222.
17. Ibid., 231.
18. Ibid.

CHAPTER FOUR
"KINGDOM OF GOD" AND HOSPITALITY TO THE STRANGER

1. See Robert Barron, *And Now I See: A Theology of Transformation* (New York: Crossroad, 1998).
2. Luke T. Johnson, "Imagining the World Scripture Imagines," *Modern Theology* 14/2 (April 1998), 166.
3. Ibid., 172.
4. Walter Wink, *When the Powers Fall: Reconciliation in the Healing of Nations* (Minneapolis, Minn.: Fortress Press, 1998), 4.
5. Ibid.
6. Johnson, *Sharing Possessions*, 65.

7. Sallie McFague, *Models of God: Theology for an Ecological Nuclear Age* (Philadelphia: Fortress Press, 1987), 173.

8. Jon Sobrino, "Central Position of the Reign of God in Liberation Theology," in *Systematic Theology*, ed. Jon Sobrino and Ignacio Ellacuría (Maryknoll, N.Y.: Orbis Books, 1996), 48.

9. Johnson, *Sharing Possessions*, 40.

10. Robert Bellah, "Liturgy and Experience," in *The Roots of Ritual*, ed. James Shaugnessy (Grand Rapids, Mich.: Eerdmans, 1973), 232.

11. Monika Hellwig, *The Eucharist* (Kansas City, Mo.: Sheed and Ward, 1992), 18.

12. Ibid., 70.

13. Johnson, *Sharing Possessions*, 104–5.

14. Palmer, *The Company of Strangers*, 35.

15. James Loder, *The Transforming Moment,* quoted in Koenig, *New Testament Hospitality*, 116.

16. Victor Codina, "Sacraments," in *Mysterium Liberationis: Fundamental Concepts of Liberation Theology*, ed. Ignacio Ellacuría and Jon Sobrino (Maryknoll, N.Y.: Orbis Books, 1993), 672.

CHAPTER FIVE
THE GOD OF HOSPITALITY

1. Johnson, "Imagining the World Scripture Imagines," 176.

2. Karl Rahner, *Foundations of Christian Faith: An Introduction to the Idea of Christianity* (New York: Seabury Press, 1978), 44.

3. Karl Rahner, "The Festival of the Future of the World," *Theological Investigations* 7 (New York: Seabury, 1977), 183–84.

4. Johnson, *Sharing Possessions*, 79.

5. Jon Sobrino, *Jesus in Latin America* (Maryknoll, N.Y.: Orbis Books, 1987), 145–46.

6. John Meier, *A Marginal Jew: Rethinking the Historical Jesus* (New York: Doubleday, 1991), 8.

7. Walter Kasper, *The God of Jesus Christ* (New York: Crossroad, 1984), 172.

8. Dorothy Lee-Pollard, "Powerlessness as Power: A Key to Emphasis in the Gospel of Mark," *Scottish Journal of Theology* 40 (1987), 185.

9. Rollo May, *Power and Innocence* (New York: Norton, 1972), 105.

10. Nathan Mitchell, *Real Presence: The Work of the Eucharist* (Chicago: Liturgy Training Publications, 1998), 46.

11. Kasper, *The God of Jesus Christ*, 172.

12. Jürgen Moltmann, "Theology in the Project of the Modern World," in *A Passion for God's Reign: Theology, Christian Learning and the Christian Self*, ed. Jürgen Moltmann, Nicholas Woltersturff, and Ellen T. Charry (Grand Rapids, Mich.: Eerdmans, 1998), 17.

13. Koenig, *New Testament Hospitality*, 59.

14. Jürgen Moltmann, *The Spirit of Life: A Universal Affirmation* (Minneapolis, Minn.: Fortress Press, 1993), 118.

15. Christopher Moody, *Eccentric Ministry* (London: Darton, Longman, and Todd, 1987), 132.

16. Johnson, "Imagining the World Scripture Imagines," 177.

CONCLUSION

1. Johnson, "Imagining the World Scripture Imagines," 177.

Other Robert J. Wicks Spirituality Selections

Simply SoulStirring by Francis Dorff, O. Praem.
Transforming Fire by Kathleen Fischer